WOULD **YOU** DATE YOU?

SONIA HARRIS

ISBN.13: 978-1-728723-76-1

Cover design by: Tiny Designs Ltd

Printed in the United Kingdom

THIS BOOK IS DEDICATED TO:

GOD
You constantly remind me that all things are possible
because you are my strength.

ROB
I am who I am because you cover me.

OUR BOYS
Keep watching and listening.
You will see the need and hear your instruction.

CONTENTS

FOREWORD

You have done it again! Two books published in four months! A typical example of who you are and what you can achieve. When I reflect on the embryonic conversations we had about this material (for the course) and what it would take to make it a reality, I am astounded by the ability that you have to produce and create things, whilst being an amazing wife and companion, mother to our amazing sons (who constantly demand your attention), role model and life coach to so many woman of all ages and juggle the various roles you currently fulfil. They surely do not make them like you anymore! I truly believe you are in a season of plenty and I am honored to share this season with you. I look forward to many more experiences with you, now and in the future.

Although I have had some input into this project and we have delivered this material on numerous occasions together, it was still a struggle to put this book down. Despite being married to you for so long, reading the words on the pages made me reflect on myself (again) and self-analyze *what needs to give, what needs to go & what needs to grow?* To enable me to be a better husband, father and friend.

This is a must read for single or dating individuals but also any person who desires to experience a relationship the way God has designed relationships to be. In John 10:10, Jesus says that, 'The enemy comes to steal, kill and destroy!' and this is so true of many relationships, even Christian ones. I strongly believe that this book is designed to assist in the reality of the second part of that scripture, 'Jesus comes that they may have life and that they may have it more abundantly.' I can testify that, living by and chasing after the principles in this book and seeking to follow Him will allow you to 'have life more abundantly' – especially in the area of relationships.

On behalf of myself and our boys, 'we love you' and are so very proud of you, AGAIN……..

Rob Harris

This brilliant book is an honest and raw look into becoming *rooted* and grounded in God. The book is real and provides you with a rare insight into a couple's personal journey into becoming individually whole and ready for their journey to marriage.

It is insightful, encouraging and hopeful whilst thought-provoking and challenging. Its triumph is in providing you with practical tools to take you on your personal journey and the simple tips that you can use again and again as you walk this road.

Having read the first book, which made me cry and laugh out loud, this book did not disappoint. I took a longer and refreshed look at where I was and have found it an essential part of my continued self-reflection and growth.

Enjoy the read, take your time and I know you will be changed......if you choose to be.

Juliet Bates, Experiential & Sports Marketing Manager, BMW

I've had the privilege of being Rob and Sonia's pastor for the past 19 years. They came to City Gates Church within a year of each other and they were both pretty 'broken'. They planted themselves in the church and from that time they have truly flourished.

Individually I could see that they had a desire to mentor people and as they came together in marriage I saw that desire develop, particularly in the area of relationships. Eventually, *Rooted* was birthed.

Rob & Sonia have held the *Rooted* course several times at City Gates and every time it has been very well attended – which is a true indication that there is a need for this type of teaching within the wider church. They have certainly found a niche!

I have spoken to people of all ages who have attended the *Rooted* course and I can truly say that many have been transformed through Sonia & Rob's teaching, and their ministry.

I'm so excited that they have decided to write this book because I believe that this will prove to be very effective for those who read it.

I would highly recommend this book to anyone who has a desire to have a healthy relationship with others.

Sonia's first book was captivating and once I started to read it I couldn't put it down! It assisted me - not just as a pastor, but also as an individual, to seek the Lord and also to put some of the mechanisms stated in the book into practice – helping me to relate to others.

Pastor Stephen Derbyshire - Senior Pastor, City Gates Church

ACKNOWLEDGMENTS

Franki
He told you to tell me that I would write, but it
would be *truth.*

Here it is!

To all those, past and present who believed in me,
prayed for me and spoke encouraging words over
me.

It worked!

Thank you!

INTRODUCTION

In my previous book I left you with a question – 'Would you date you?'

Most people that have attended the *Rooted for Relationships* course have, at the very least, pondered on that question, and, at most, changed one or two (or many things) about themselves after some self-reflection.

In seeking that special someone, we tend to focus on them, that person we would like to meet one day – good points and bad points. We do not, however, tend to analyze ourselves quite so much, and our friends and family are often too kind to tell us that we are being unreasonable, neurotic, possessive, obsessive, rude, argumentative, selfish or single-minded. They either love us too much or they've become used to it.

Either way we roll along in our cocoon of splendor and never take a good, long, hard look at ourselves.

The focus of the *Rooted for Relationships* course (or *Rooted*, as it has become known) is just that. Taking an inward look at you, and being prayerful about what needs to give, what needs to go, and what needs to grow.

So, are you ready to take a look in the mirror to see what you find?

1
YOUR WAY OR GOD'S WAY?

Whilst this book is not written with the aim that you will be in a relationship by the time you reach the last chapter, I do appreciate that the reason you are reading this book is because you would like, at some point, to be in a relationship that will eventually lead to marriage – ideally a successful marriage that will be purposeful, powerful and plentiful. I can't make that happen for you. No-one can. But I will attempt to assist with the journey and process of preparing you so that the package you present is favorable.

As my husband Rob and I present the course together, I will include his views, knowledge, wisdom and testimonies as you will benefit from what he has to say – I certainly do.

So, dating.

This means different things to different people.

Some see dating as an opportunity to spend one to one time with someone else to ascertain whether they would like to take things further. Others have told us that dating is the more serious 'boyfriend and girlfriend stage'. Some have described it as preparation for marriage. Some say it is an opportunity to 'see' different people - to sample a variety of what is on offer and make a choice based on their findings.

Dating for others is a commitment to be together, sometimes for many years, and building a life together. This may involve co-habiting, sex, shared finances and children. There are other views also, depending on who you speak to but those above are generally the responses we get as we open up the microphone to delegates and allow them to give us insight into their thoughts, views and lifestyles.

What we will not do on the *Rooted* course is enforce our views upon anyone and sometimes we remain neutral, allowing others to conclude for themselves as we appreciate that one size does not fit all. However, what we do do throughout the course is communicate what God's Word has to say about a given topic, subject or matter.

In biblical times, a woman was brought to a man, having been prepared and chosen as suitable for him. He would 'lay' with her and she would become his wife.

Whilst the marriage ceremony has somewhat changed over the years, the law hasn't. It is still recognized today that; a marriage is not legally binding unless is has been consummated. If the married couple have not consummated the marriage, the marriage can be annulled. More on this later, but you get the idea.

Dating in today's society has become multi-faceted with varying stages but in biblical times it was not like that at all. In the book of Esther, you will see that the king was able to take his pick from a large selection of beautiful ladies, however, the average man did not have these options. Maybe, in this day and age, we have adopted the rights of biblical kings to pick and choose and sample before deciding on 'the one'. Unfortunately, we have also adopted the concubine creed – let's not go there, yet!

Question:

✏️ What three 'things' are *essential* to you when dating? (Essential, not just desirable)

1.	
2.	
3.	

Have a think and write these down.

Bear in mind, we are talking about dating here, not marriage. Does that make a difference? Would your answers change if we *were* asking about marriage?

Bear these answers in mind as we continue on and see whether they change as you progress through the book.

Now, let's look at these questions:

What do you expect out of a relationship?

Where did your expectations come from?

What if your expectations are misguided?

You may not choose to write down answers to these questions, but certainly have a think about them. *What do you expect from a relationship, and why?* That may seem like a strange question, but we want you to think about your expectations.

For example, I once spent time with a guy who didn't own a car and didn't feel the need to own a car, as he lived in London. He was happy to take public transport wherever he needed to go. On more than one occasion having spent time in central London or the West End together, I found myself on the night bus with him, coming home in the early hours of the morning. The night bus was not a pleasant experience for me but to make matters worse, he would disembark quite some time before I would (as I lived further away from Central London than he did), which left me walking, alone, through the dark streets (once, with my shoes off so as not to make it obvious that a young woman was walking alone and was potential, easy prey).

If you had asked me then, you can bet I would have listed *a car* as essential – *and* it would have been essential that the car door would be held open for me each and every time I entered or exited the vehicle. Would I list that as essential now? Probably not. It is not high on my list of requirements because my circumstances have changed.

Do you expect a man to always pay when you go out? Do you expect a lady to let you choose the wine? Do you expect to be collected from your home when you arrange to go out or are you happy to meet at the venue? Do you expect to always pray before you eat? Do you expect to end every date in prayer? Does she have to be a vegetarian because you are?

Our expectations are so vast and varied, but some are consistent when we ask delegates to share what they have written: *'He/She has to be a Christian'*. Can I pause on this one? We are going to do an exercise later in this chapter which will elaborate on that point so let's park that one for now.

Let's look at question b). *Where did your expectations come from?*

One thing that sticks out in my mind with regards to this question, was a movie I watched back when I was single. I no longer wanted to be single and some days were harder than others. This movie was about a young man who made a bet that he could date and keep a woman. The woman however was writing an article about how to make a man 'run a mile.' So, he was trying to keep her, she was trying to get rid of him. He was going all out to 'woo' this lady.

Meanwhile, I'm watching this movie and he is wooing *me*. I was ready to pack my bags and move to LA, or at least visit, in an attempt to find a man that would treat me *'like that'*. You may laugh, but the images and perceptions on the Hollywood screen often build a misguided reality in the minds of those who long for love. Media is a great deceiver of the mind and no matter how much we know it to be fake, we still long for it to be true. And yet, in the movies, no-one has scars or blemishes, no-one has morning breath, and no-one wears mismatched underwear!

You may also find yourself observing someone else's relationship and wishing it was your own. Whilst that is admirable and encouraging to know that there are good role models out there, a word of caution; only God truly knows what goes on in the hearts, minds and homes of those we only see on Sundays. Also, they may be carrying a burden that you really don't want to own. I have learned not to idolize other people and covet what they have (or appear to have) but I do glean from wise council and elements of what I see in others, i.e. kindness, generosity, patience, self-control, humility etc.

My constant prayer is that I will be changed by God, to be more like the person He created me to be, and less like the person I used to be.

By all means, have a plan and a vision for your relationship but have the wisdom and flexibility to learn as you go. It's not *all* about you anymore.

Standards

Now, before you even think about getting into a/another relationship, let's take a look at your standards. We all have standards – even if you've not thought about them or realized you have some, I can assure you – you do.

Many of us would have had standards instilled in us by our parents or those we grew up with. 'Say *please!*' 'Eat with your mouth closed!' 'Stand, when the head teacher enters the room.' These are all standards, expectations, if you like, of what you should and should not do. As we grow and gain independence, we begin to set standards for ourselves. These become guidelines for us as they *guide* our behavior and set limitations that keep us safe and comfortable. These standards can be unique to us as individuals or more widely known and recognized within a certain culture or demographic. Whichever the case, we have them.

Ponder on what your standards are. It's important to know them. Keep them in mind as we now look at boundaries.

Boundaries

Boundaries are more applicable to a situation than to the individual. Boundaries are used to set limitations, and so, in a relationship you will have boundaries around the 'do's and don'ts of your relationship.' For example, you may both decide you will not speak on the phone after a certain time or you may decide not to spend more than a certain amount on any item of clothing as you are saving for your wedding. Whatever it may be, it should be something you decide and agree on together – although you may find that one has to enforce the boundary when the other is weak or struggling.

Standards and boundaries are much like a set of rules. Rules set to protect you and your relationship. Standards should be set and in place *before* dating begins. Boundaries should be in place to guide you *during* dating, and beyond. You and your partner need a benchmark to work with. The bible states, in 1 Corinthians 10:23, *'Everything is permissible, but not everything is beneficial.'* In order for you and your partner to know the limitations there has to be standards and boundaries.

Another word of caution; please refrain from being or becoming judgmental of others if their standards are different to yours. Standards are a set of reminders to prevent you from compromising what you believe or know to be true. They are not a tool or weapon to be used to make others feel uncomfortable or insignificant.

🌩 Remember: **If you stand for nothing, you'll fall for anything.**

Don't be dissuaded about what you *know* to be true. People can only deceive you if you are unsure. I was told many years ago; 'if you don't know, get to know'.

Self-Analysis

We are now going to do a self-analysis exercise.

Just as Esther and Daniel in the Bible had a time of preparation, we too should take the opportunity to prepare ourselves for the 'gift' (husband or wife) that God will present to you one day.

How many of us have been given a gift and felt disappointed when we have opened it? We may not show the disappointment, but maybe, deep down, we were hoping for something different.

When you meet someone, the 'packaging' may look great but as you look deeper into that 'package' you may begin to feel disappointed. As we go through this self-analysis, please bear in mind that *you* are someone's gift and they will want to open that package and discover what is inside. Will they be disappointed?

Let's delve in;

Christian?

So, you call yourself a Christian? You state on your 'list' of requirements that he/she must also be a Christian. But let's take a closer look at *you*.

Being a Christian can often be a label that we wear, and, let's be honest, we sometimes/often take the label off when it suits us, and put it back on as we approach the entrance of our church building.

Being raised in church or 'dragged along' as a child doesn't qualify us to use the term Christian – neither does carrying the biggest, leather bound bible, displayed for all to see. For some, being born in the UK justifies being 'branded' as a

Christian. 'It's a Christian country, I was born here, that makes me a Christian, right?' Well, would that be sufficient for you in a partner?

Rob and I spend a lot of our time mentoring others, especially in the area of relationships. When one of our mentees informs us that they have 'met someone', and we ask whether the person is a Christian – if we hear that high-pitched, 'Well.......', accompanied by the roll of the eyes and the head tipped to one side, we have our answer. The 'well....' is usually closely followed by, 'He grew up in church but isn't connected to a church right now, BUT he prays all the time and he knows scripture!' Sound familiar to you?

The other explanation we hear is, 'No, but she's very interested in coming to church with me and says she is free three Sundays from now and every other month!'

The thing is, you don't need to convince *us* of anything. You just need to remember what the Bible says about being unequally yoked and take a snapshot of your life 10 years from now and see whether you like what you see. Don't get me wrong, it could all work out fine. She could get saved and be dynamic for God. But do you want to take the risk? There are ministries within churches that are specifically for spouses with unsaved partners. Some of those spouses have been members for many, many years. They didn't necessarily marry unsaved partners. Some of them gave their lives to Christ after they were already married but their partners are yet to follow. What will your story be?

 Read 2 Cor 6:14-18 and decide for yourself.

Have you actually made a commitment to Christ yourself? Are you living a Christ-filled life? Have you been baptized?

 Read 2 Cor 5:17.

This means that anyone who belongs to Christ has become a new person. The old life is gone; a new life has begun.

If you are seeking a Godly partner to become your

spouse, ensure you are also endeavoring to be that which you are seeking.

Studying the Word

Any relationship, in any form, whether it be a romantic relationship, family, friendship, work colleagues – these all take time and effort to develop. Let's use friendship as an example. When you meet someone for the first time, you may exchange small talk to begin with. That small talk may develop into deeper conversation with jokes being shared or personal information being exchanged. At this stage the relationship could go either way. It could all end there, as a one-off conversation or you may decide to continue the friendship and meet for coffee etc. What generally transpires if you decide to go with the latter is that you will begin to show interest in that person's life. You will spend time talking and hanging out with them. You check out their social media, exchange photos, hang out with each other and introduce them to family and other friends. Generally, you will get to know them better. You may even find yourself becoming a little more like them; using the same terminology, displaying the same body language and so on.

In our relationship with Christ, one of the ways we get to know Him is by reading His word. The bible consists of 'stories' of Christ and the history that led up to Christ being on earth. As we read it, it pieces together and answers many of the questions we will invariably have, not just about Him but also about us. It answers the why's and the who's. The when, where and what's will also become clearer and the how begins to reveal itself via the Holy Spirit.

In short, we are building a relationship with Christ by getting to know Him through His word.

To maintain any good friendship there needs to be regular contact and a sharing of information. Being up to date with what is going on with your friend will allow you to *know* them better; on a deeper level.

In the same way we must maintain a strong friendship with Christ and that requires regular reading of His word. The more you read the Bible the more you learn and understand the content. Very soon you will be able memorize particular verses of the Bible and these will be an encouragement, not only to you but to others.

We you pray using scripture from the bible, you are speaking God's language!

In Matthew 4:1-11 we see a conversation taking place between Jesus and Satan. They both use scripture to communicate. Satan tries to tempt Jesus by using scripture to entice Him. Jesus rebukes Satan, again using scripture. Eventually Satan gives up and leaves Jesus to be tended to by angels.

Scripture is Christ's language. Learn it, use it, understand it. It will draw you closer to God.

Fruits of the Spirit

In Galatians, chapter 5, verses 22-23 the fruits of the Spirit are listed as a guide to how we should live. These nine qualities should ideally be displayed as we carry the mantle of being children of God.

Love, Joy, Peace, Patience, Kindness, Goodness, Faithfulness, Gentleness and Self Control are what we should be emitting as we go about our daily lives. But look at this portion of scripture which is quoted just prior to the listing of the fruits of the Spirit;

So I say, let the Holy Spirit guide your lives. Then you won't be doing what your sinful nature craves. The sinful nature wants to do evil, which is just the opposite of what the Spirit wants. And the Spirit gives us desires that are the opposite of what the sinful nature desires. These two forces are constantly fighting each other, so you are not free to carry out your good intentions. But when you are directed by the Spirit, you are not under obligation to the law of Moses.

When you follow the desires of your sinful nature, the results are very clear: sexual immorality, impurity, lustful pleasures, idolatry, sorcery, hostility, quarrelling, jealousy, outbursts of anger, selfish ambition, dissension, division, envy, drunkenness, wild parties, and other sins like these. Let me tell you again, as I have before, that anyone living that sort of life will not inherit the Kingdom of God.

Gal 5:16-21 (NLT)

Quite often this bit gets missed, possibly because it's quite hard hitting, but we should take heed to all of it – not just the nice bit. It's always better to have the full picture, even if the picture is a little scary.

Verse 17 advises us that the two forces are constantly fighting each other, which means, it's not going to be easy to display the fruits as you go about your daily life – but it is possible.

Are there any that you particularly struggle with?

John 15:4 (NLT) tells us how we can produce this fruit:

> *Remain in me, and I will remain in you. For a*
> *branch cannot produce fruit if it is severed from*
> *the vine, and you cannot be fruitful unless you*
> *remain in me.*

Prayerful

Just as communication and conversation are essential to building and maintaining friendships, prayer is the communication and conversation between you and God.

Are you:

- ☐ Spending daily time in prayer?
- ☐ Talking to God?
- ☐ Praying for others?
- ☐ Giving thanks?
- ☐ Hearing from God?
- ☐ Receiving your instructions?
- ☐ Worshipping?

All of the above will allow you to build an intimate relationship with God.

Remember, prayer is not an exercise in reciting scripted words to God and rushing on with your day. Prayer is a conversation with God. This may mean sharing what is on your heart, your thoughts, your fears, your highs and your lows. Asking for help for others, giving thanks for what

God has done or simply adoration for who He is. It may also be questions and requests for guidance.

However you choose to pray, remember that it doesn't have to be hours and hours of repetitive talking and pleading:

> *When you pray, don't babble on and on as the Gentiles do. They think their prayers are answered merely by repeating their words again and again.*
>
> **Matthew 6:7 (NLT)**

Just let God hear your heart and take time to listen to what He has to say. Remember, a friendship where you just talk and talk and talk, and never listen, is probably not going to be a healthy one.

Whilst you are single, bear this in mind:

> *32 I want you to be free from the concerns of this life. An unmarried man can spend his time doing the Lord's work and thinking how to please him. 33 But a married man has to think about his earthly responsibilities and how to please his wife. 34 His interests are divided. In the same way, a woman who is no longer married or has never been married can be devoted to the Lord and holy in body and in spirit. But*

a married woman has to think about her earthly responsibilities and how to please her husband.

1 Cor 7:32-34 (NLT)

I had read this passage of scripture many, many times whilst I was single. I didn't ignore it. It made perfect sense. But I didn't realize just how true it was until I was actually married.

Instantly, my prayer life changed. I became very aware that my prayers could be overheard – even if Rob was asleep or out, I was always mindful that he may wake up or come home and listen in on my private 'sessions' with God. You see, my prayers had become very personal and intimate with God when I was single. I would share my innermost thoughts and feelings; my fears and my struggles. I would weep sometimes. At other times I would laugh uncontrollably. Occasionally I would find myself laying prostrate on the floor, deep in prayer, and remain there for a long time.

Can you imagine the scene if Rob came into the room where I was praying and found me in any one of those aforementioned states? Now, I know that he would understand, but back then, I didn't know what he would think or feel.

I would encourage you to find *your* way of spending time with God, but can I suggest that your prayer time is not always fleeting or slotted in to whatever else you have going on. By this, I mean, reading on the train on the way to work or a quick prayer before you jump out of bed in the morning. Those times are important, but I invite you to spend prolonged time with God. Go in! I find that when I have extended prayer time I transform from a place of speaking and acknowledgement to a realm of intersession, warfare, gratitude and revelation. And it doesn't always look pretty. It doesn't always sound attractive either. On one occasion, whilst in my bedroom, on my knees, praying in tongues, unbeknown to me one of my children came into the room and heard me. He promptly ran downstairs to Rob and declared, "Daddy, Mummy is upstairs on the floor speaking funny!" Rob knew I was praying so he wasn't alarmed. Later, my son asked me, "Mummy, I didn't know you could speak different languages?" I smiled at him and tried to explain 'tongues' to him. I think he got it.

The majority of my instructions from God, especially those that involve a change in direction or an action or instruction, have followed extended prayer times. I must add, I also hear from God a lot when I'm in the shower! This book is the result of an internal conversation with God in the shower. I asked God how we (Rob & I) could reach more people with the teaching from *Rooted.* His answer was, 'write it down'. Now, this resonated with me. I'll tell you why.

Many years ago, I was working at a temporary job in London. I had nothing to do all day, but they wanted to keep me there as back up to the PA of the Chairman and Chief executive. I had been hired to cover her annual leave weeks before and I guess they were happy with my work, so they wanted to keep me on site in case the PA fell ill or took more annual leave. At first, it sounded like a dream – getting paid to do nothing! But, very quickly, I became bored, unchallenged and restless. One day I opened a word document and began to type. Before I knew it, I had written several chapters. I started with what I could see out of the 6th floor window and the rest just flooded out. One Sunday, at church, after the morning service, I was having a conversation with a lady who was my home group leader. I told her I had been writing and I asked if I could send the chapters I had written to her. She agreed, and we went our separate ways.

Later that same day, following the evening service, she came to me and took me to one side. She looked at me intensely and said, "Sonia, I read what you have written and then I prayed. I asked God why you had given me this piece of work to read, seeing as we are not that close. God told me to tell you, 'You will write, but it will be truth'". In that moment, I knew my next move.

The next day, back at work, I opened the document. I highlighted all of the text - title and everything. Without hesitation, I hit *delete* and then I hit *save*. It was gone.

It was not a wasted exercise. I had also sent the unfinished manuscript to my sister. She called me after reading it and said, "You do realize that this is you!" I asked her what she meant. She went on to explain that as she read the chapters she could see that the main character was me – even down to the clothing I had described in detail – she believed it was me! I hadn't seen it. I thought I had created a fictional character but, in fact, I had described *me*. I didn't realize that that was what I was doing but my sister, who knows me well, had identified it. It dawned on me that what I had been writing was actually a fictional story but with a very real *me* as the main character. But it was the old me. In deleting the content, I was saying goodbye to the old me. It was a cleansing exercise. I was now looking ahead. I was ready to move forward.

Years later, I'm talking approx. 16 years later, I'm in the shower and God tells me to write that 'truth'. In obedience I began to write and the introduction to this book became *PlusOne = 3*, my first book. So, now, I'm writing this book in an attempt to put the teaching from the *Rooted* course on paper. The power of prayer!

Good Steward

God gives us responsibility. Everything we have, He has given us. What do you do with it?

Time – Do you use your time wisely? It is very tempting to spend your evenings watching box sets or reality TV or sport. But is that the best use of time? What else could you be doing? Could you learn a trade or study for a degree? Could you volunteer? Could you serve in ministry? Could you babysit for someone who needs it? Could you do your elderly neighbors' shopping? Could you clean your house, or someone else's? There is so much you could do. Relaxation and reflection time is so important. So is sleep. But if you are squandering time doing nothing important – that is a waste. Be careful not to fall into temptation because you have nothing to do. The internet can be a dangerous place when you spend hours searching and searching with no particular goal in mind.

Money – What do you spend your money on?

You? Well, you've earned it, so you have the right to spend it on yourself, right? Right! But, we are called to give to those in need.

> ³² All the believers were united in heart and mind. And they felt that what they owned was not their own, so they shared everything they had. ³³ The apostles testified powerfully to the resurrection of the Lord Jesus, and God's great blessing was upon them all. ³⁴ There were no needy people among them, because those who owned land or houses would sell them ³⁵ and bring the money to the apostles to give to those in need.

Acts 4:32-35 (NLT)

Those in need are not just the homeless and charities overseas. The person sitting or living next to you may be in need. Can you help them? We can all reach a time of hardship at some stage in our lives. Whether it's £10 or £100 or £1000, God has given us all the ability to help others.

Don't forget your local church. Have you ever sat in church on a Sunday and thought, 'It's a bit cold in here?' Well, maybe they can't afford to heat the building because the only income they get to pay for heating and lighting and food and toilet roll is what you give. Next time you sip that free coffee think about who paid for it!

Gifts – We all have a particular gift. I'm not talking about a present, I'm talking about a particular ability or specialty that has been given to us by God. Do you know what yours is? There are assessments and tests that will help you to ascertain this. Thankfully, I discovered mine early on in my Christian walk, but I have to say I wasn't pleased when I discovered what my primary gift is. This may seem odd, but I didn't understand it.

At my church, when I first became a Christian, I was invited to attend the Network course. The Network Course enabled attendees to identify what their spiritual gift was. At the time, my mind was set on becoming a foster carer. I had been approved and was quite a way along in the process. I completed the assessment part of the Network course and the outcome shocked me. Others had also calculated their results and prophecy, healing, hospitality, missionary and evangelist were all declared aloud as the course leaders asked us to share our findings. When my time came to announce my primary gifting, I almost whispered it. My primary gift was *Administration*.

At the time, I understood administration to mean, paperwork, typing and spreadsheets - so you can understand my confusion and disappointment when I discovered that God had given me *that* as a 'gift'. In my mind, everyone does that. There was nothing special whatsoever about it and it certainly didn't feel like a gift! I resolved that the results must have been incorrect and vowed to repeat the assessment again at home. I did, and the results were the same. My coping strategy was to park the whole exercise and frankly ignore it. God had other plans.

Soon afterwards, I began getting more and more involved in church activity and I naturally became the planner and organizer. I even joined the choir – those of you that have heard me sing would agree that I wasn't there for my harmonies or solos. Whilst I am not tone deaf, am I not a vocalist by any stretch of the imagination, yet there I was, grouped with the altos, adding bulk and volume to the far more able singers. When I look back, I know my purpose for being a part of that ministry was to plan and organize the mission trips and events that we did throughout that time. The worship leader was merciful and allowed me to stand at the back and work my two-step, but he knew what God knew – it just hadn't registered with me yet.

It was when I began working for my church as the pastoral team PA that I really began to see my giftings materialize. My pastor said to me, after a few weeks of employment, 'Sonia, you have a gift!' I looked at him, puzzled. Again, for my sake, he repeated, 'You have a gift. A gift of administration. You don't see it, but I do.' That's when it hit home for me. Slowly, I began to embrace it and as I looked more deeply into when the gift meant, I understood, and more importantly, recognized the qualities that were displaying themselves as I continued on my journey of Christianity.

Make every effort to discover what your gifts are – you are probably already operating in them without realizing it. Don't waste time trying to perfect your weaknesses. Work to your strengths and let others work to theirs. Collaborate with others when needed and know enough to not get cheated - but your gift will empower you, both in ministry and business.

Passion – What gets you excited? What makes you angry? What brings tears to your eyes? What would you do without being paid to do it? What types of people stir up your compassion? These questions will help you to know what your purpose is. It may not come to you like a thunderbolt, but you will gradually gravitate towards those areas where you feel a sense of compassion or knowledge or duty.

Being a good steward means not just griping about the things that make you angry or frustrated - act upon it! Do something! And, don't just pray about it, take action. Make a call, write an email, feed someone who is hungry, listen to someone who is lonely, buy a gift for a child who doesn't have much, assist a working mum who needs help to collect her children from school. Do something! The smallest act of kindness will show a stranger or friend the heart of Christ.

Children – Children are a gift from God. Whether they are yours or someone else's, they are a gift. If they have been given to you, understand that it is your responsibly, whether you are a parent or a teacher, to care for them and help them feel safe and loved. Having a child entrusted into your care is an enormous responsibility. It's ok to get it wrong whilst trying to get it right. None of us are perfect. But, be prepared to learn and be ready to change if it means you become that better carer to that child. The way you care for them will shape the person they become as adults. The way you parent them influences the way they will parent their own children. Let that influence be positive.

People – People will be placed in your care, even for a fleeting moment. What impression will you leave on them. Above all, please remember that you carry the light of Christ wherever you go. If others see misery, moaning and manipulation they will not desire a life with Christ – and certainly not a life with you!

Have you ever been around someone who, every time you great them, their response is, 'I'm tired'. We all get tired from time to time, but, *every time!?* I find people like that draining. They make me feel low and effortless. By the time I'm done talking with them *I* want to sleep too! It may be that they are genuinely tired but as a non-Christian, I would not be drawn to the life of Christianity if that is what it looked like.

Be a good steward of what God has given you. Each one of us has been given a measure of the above categories. If God can trust you with the time, money, gifts, passion, children and people He has placed in your life, He will continue to add to you and use you for His glory.

[10] *"If you are faithful in little things, you will be*

faithful in large ones. But if you are dishonest in little things, you won't be honest with greater responsibilities.

Luke 16:10 (NLT)

What an honor!

Serving

Are you serving in the kingdom of God?
Are you serving in your community?
Are you serving at home?
Are you serving at work?

Serving can often be identified as those who steward people to their seats at a meeting or those that serve coffee following a meeting. But serving comes in many forms. In my church, there is a man whose profession is a window cleaner. His way of serving is to clean the church windows for free. Can I add that my church consists of four floors and built of pure glass! Our pastor has offered, many times, to pay him for his services. He refuses. That is his way of serving his local church. Many years ago, whilst in our previous church building, there was an alleyway that led to the back of the church. There were wooden gates that were to be closed and locked at the end of the day, but they would often be left open. Being located in the centre of town there would be 'night time activity' that would take place long after you and I were tucked up in bed. One of our members took it upon himself to come in early in the morning, before the pastor and other staff members arrived, to clear away beer cans, bottles, needles and condoms from the site. That was his ministry. I could go on to name a wide variety of ways that the members of our church serve, but you get the gist, don't you?

In our communities and workplaces, we can reflect Christ by going beyond the ordinary or expected. Let our neighbors see something more than a nod or wave. Offer to help. Stop for a chat. Buy two and *give* one free. Mowing the front lawn? Offer to do theirs whilst the lawnmower is out. Walk their dog whilst you walk yours. Watch their kids or let them join your kids for that day out. Buy your work colleague a costa coffee whilst you purchase yours. Share some doughnuts. Do the photocopying if he/she is inundated with work.

Standing in judgement and telling people what they shouldn't be doing *does not* reflect Christ. Ideally, you want to be drawing people closer, not making them run a mile or avoid you completely. Let's reserve the scriptures for the services and prayer meetings and just show love to those who need it – which, technically, is all of us, right?

At home, outdo each other with love, kind words and gestures. Rob always asks me in the morning, 'How did you sleep?' It feels good. Now, I ask my children, 'How did you sleep'. Leadership influence. Rob will text me throughout his day when we are not together. It feels wonderful to know he is thinking of me, even when he is busy doing other things. I reflect that behavior and do the same. I have learnt to communicate with Rob whenever the thought of him pops into my head. I tell him I miss him even when he is coming home a few hours later.

He likes it. I like it. It's our way of serving each other. Around the house, we push ourselves to ensure tasks are completed because it will make 'the other one' happy. It works. Try it.

When it comes to serving, you may not know what it is that you are good at or what interests you but there is always something to be done. Get involved and you will see your giftings and passions materialize through serving others.

Appearance

Generally, when we give gifts to our friends and loved ones, we go to great lengths to present them nicely. The wrapping is almost as important as the actual gift inside. The wrapping adds an air of mystery and anticipation. The excitement of what may be inside builds and builds - until the moment of reveal. The gift looks attractive. It draws you to it. Even as children we feel this way – and it doesn't change as we develop into adults.

If we desire to be in a relationship we too are preparing to present ourselves to someone as a gift. We want that person to find us attractive, to be excited about what they will 'get'.

None of us are perfect. We all have flaws and 'bits' that we don't like about ourselves. Irrespective of those things, we should make every effort to 'wrap' ourselves nicely and be ready to be presented to someone.

Now, let me clarify. I am not talking about vanity here. Neither am I saying that you should be made up like a show horse all day, every day. I am simply saying make an effort and cover the basics. I won't list the basics because they are different for each person (I have come to realize that). I once shared in a session (Pre-marriage course) that I shower and apply perfume as part of my preparation for bed. One young lady thought this was bizarre and explained that she thought it was a lot of effort and unsustainable. I realized at that point that everyone has a different level of self-care.

When you enter into a relationship you become a part of that person and you represent them even when you are not intentionally 'on show'. When you both go out to meet with friends or attend a wedding together you will make every effort to present yourselves nicely. However, if you are popping into the high street for supplies you may not bother. Let's imagine you bump into your partner's cousin and you are looking (or smelling) less than your best. What thoughts could be running through that cousin's mind? And will he or she just be thinking of you, or will they be trying to empathize with their cousin who married you.

Even at home, especially when married couples get comfortable with each other, things can become, let's call it, *relaxed*. Those 'house clothes' that have been with you since you were a teenager may need an upgrade. By all means, be comfortable but try not to turn into the scarecrow from The Wizard of Oz!

To those who feel it may be attractive and liberating to walk around the house naked – oh, this does happen – if it works for *both* of you, great. Generally, it doesn't. Nakedness during intimate moments is enticing and attractive. Nakedness whilst you empty the bins and stack the dishwasher – less so. Check with your spouse whether this works for him/her.

Finally, on this point, do your best to keep yourself healthy and respect the earthly body you have been given.

Attitude

Our attitude to life and our attitude to others will have a huge impact on our ability to influence.

Do people tend to flock to you? Do you have a lot of friends that *want* to be around you? Or, do people tend to be uncomfortable around you. Are you making others uncomfortable by the way you behave? Do you tend to see the negative in everything? Are you very intense, analyzing everything and everyone? Our attitude defines how we behave.

Look at these:

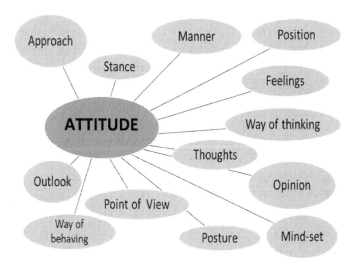

These are all *'Expressions of Attitude'*. Some are visual, some are verbal some are emotional – they all come together to form a large part of what others see when they are around you.

On a date, these expressions will display themselves and your date may decide, very quickly, whether they wish to spend any more time with you. Rightly or wrongly, your attitude, your personal expression, will allow others to form an opinion of you.

This doesn't mean you should not *be yourself*. This means you should make time to analyze yourself and see whether the attitude you display to others is appealing to you. Would you like to be on the receiving end of it? Would you be attracted or repelled by it?

Do remember that, if you are a Christian, you are a walking, talking advert for Christ. You bear His name and therefore you represent Him in all you do. If you analyze yourself and find a few elements that you do not like, hear what the bible advises:

> *'Therefore, change your hearts and stop being stubborn.'*
> **Deut 10:16 (NLT)**

Submissive

This always makes for an interesting debate! A debate that we never have enough time to explore in full. Everyone seems to have their own views on what submission means, and that is why I look to God's word for what it means because otherwise it is just an opinion.

When I met Rob and realized that this man was going to be my husband, I had a conversation with Rob as I wanted to make a few things clear. Clear for him, but also for myself. I wanted to ensure that we were in agreement about specific things before we went any further into our relationship. During a conversation regarding our future, I said to Rob, "I do not have an issue with submission. I agree with it and I am ready to do it, but can I make one thing clear? I will submit to you as long as you are submitted to God. I will not submit to foolishness!" I wanted to make it *very* clear to Rob that, if at any stage, he came away from the covering of Christ and chose to live an alternative lifestyle where Christ was not his leader, I would no longer be submitting to *that* leadership. I have always made it clear to Rob that Christ is number one for me. I put Him first and worship Him only. But I love Rob and I honor and respect him as my God given leader.

Listen to what the bible says about submission between husbands and wives:

> [21]*And further, submit to one another out of reverence for Christ.*

22 *For wives, this means submit to your husbands as to the Lord.*

23 *For a husband is the head of his wife as Christ is the head of the church. He is the Saviour of his body, the church.*

24 *As the church submits to Christ, so you wives should submit to your husbands in everything.*

25 *For husbands, this means love your wives, just as Christ loved the church. He gave up his life for her* *26* *to make her holy and clean, washed by the cleansing of God's word.* *27* *He did this to present her to himself as a glorious church without a spot or wrinkle or any other blemish. Instead, she will be holy and without fault.*

28 *In the same way, husbands ought to love their wives as they love their own bodies. For a man who loves his wife actually shows love for himself.* *29* *No one hates his own body but feeds and cares for it, just as Christ cares for the church.* *30* *And we are members of his body.*

31 *As the Scriptures say, "A man leaves his father and mother and is joined to his wife, and the two are united into one."* *32* *This is a great mystery, but it is an illustration of the way Christ and the church are one.* *33* *So again I say, each man must love his wife as he loves himself, and the wife must respect her husband.*

Eph 5:21-33 (NLT)

Verse 21 is speaking to *both* husbands and wives.

Verse 22 is speaking specifically to wives.

Many read the first part (submit to your husbands) but not the last part (as to the Lord). Before you can submit to an earthly husband, have you learnt how to first submit to God? Do you talk to God? Do you listen? Do you obey His instructions – even when you are unsure or fearful about what you are being instructed to do. Do you honor God in the way that you behave or conduct yourself? Do you represent God when you are dealing with others; at home, in your place of work, at school or university. Do you obey others that have been given the place of authority in your life, i.e. your parents, employers etc. Do you trust God?

Until you can do these things, having a husband may prove very difficult for you. Consider a marriage where you do not talk/converse/communicate with your husband effectively. Consider a marriage where you do not listen but choose to shut your husband down, refuse to discuss something and retreat to another room by yourself. Consider a marriage where your husband goes off to work in the morning and asks you to call the plumber to come and check out that dripping sound you both heard in the loft the night before. You don't bother to follow this instruction. Instead you go off to work too and put that instruction off until another time. You come home much later to find the bedroom ceiling on your bed having caved in from the flooding in the loft caused by the leaking water tank! Imagine a marriage where your husband invites you along to his work Christmas party and you behave shamefully and embarrass not just him but also yourself. Imagine a marriage where you and your husband go to a family dinner where there are parents, family and close friends attending and you disrespect his mother at the dinner table in full view of everyone. Are you beginning to see the picture? My point is, until you can learn how to submit to God first and foremost, it will be difficult to submit to a husband whom you will be required to live alongside all day, every day.

When I was being prepared for marriage, God gave me this scripture;

*'For your Maker is your husband – the Lord Almighty
is his name...'*

Isaiah 54:5 (NIV)

He also told me to be a wife before I was a wife. I didn't understand what this meant until I read the scripture above and, through prayer, began to understand what God was asking of me. You see, He knew the end from the beginning. He knew that Rob and I would serve in the marriage and relationship ministry and that we would need to represent Him through our marriage. He also knew that there were areas where I was weak as well as areas were Rob was weak and so He had to prepare us both, prior to marriage, to be ready for what was ahead. That didn't mean that we were ready and without fault. If you have read my previous book *PlusOne = 3*, you will see that we certainly struggled at the beginning of our marriage, but the tools were there, and our faith had to kick in to get us through a really tough time.

Look at the comparison in verse 23. The bible compares the role of being a husband to the role of Christ being the head of the church.

Verse 24 tells us that the church submits to Christ, so wives should submit to their husbands *in everything.*

Verses 25-27 tell us how. Husbands – pay attention here! Just as Christ loved the church and gave His life up for her (the church) to make her (the church) holy and clean – a husband should love his wife, *giving up his life for her, to make her holy and clean.* Christ did this to present the church to himself as a glorious church without a spot or wrinkle or any other blemish. Instead she (the church) would be holy and without fault.

Hear this husbands: (Verse 28) *IN THE SAME WAY,* husbands ought to love their wives. Followed by 'as they love their own bodies'. Now, let's just pause here for a moment. We are not simply talking about those Mr. Universe type guys who stand in the mirror and idolize their physique whilst preparing to go to the gym for the 10th time that week! No, let's talk about the average guy who wakes up in the morning, having given his body *rest* throughout the night. He takes a shower and *cleans* himself. He applies lotion to *care* for his skin. He has breakfast to *feed* his body and *energize* himself for the morning ahead. He *clothes* himself to *present* himself suitable for the task ahead. Let's stop there...

Before this man has even left the house in the morning he has *rested, cleansed, cared, feed, energized, clothed* and *presented* himself. The word says a husband ought to love his wife as he loves his own body (verse 28). So, this means, his wife should be *rested, cleansed, cared for, feed, energized, clothed* and *presented.* Whilst I could give you a list of what that could look like, I won't. This is something to discover for yourselves in marriage as you grow together and discover more about each other. Your likes and dislikes will be different to other married couples and whilst it is fine to glean from others, always be mindful that you are different. Your marriage is unique to the two of you and you should mold it according to your preferences. Never copy or idolize someone else's marriage. You are not married to the that man or woman, you are married to your wife or your husband, and – you *chose* to be! Make your own marriage work by working at it!

I'll end this section by saying, submission is not

weakness. Submission is strength! It takes more strength to submit than it does to react, respond, lash out, disobey etc.

As we have seen, submission is not just applicable to women in marriage. We must all submit to God first and foremost.

'In all your ways submit to him and he will make your paths straight'

Prov 3:6 (NIV)

'Submit to God, and you will have peace; then things will go well for you.

Job 22:21 (NLT)

Under Authority

Are you somebody who struggles with authority? Be honest! Many of us do. Of course, much of this is dependent on the type or level of authority, or who is taking charge.

As a single person, it is easier to dictate your own schedule, so adjusting to having someone else in your life that wants to take control, or even just making suggestions can be a big adjustment.

If you are particularly resistant to coming under the authority of others, it is worth asking yourself a few exploratory questions:

Why do I struggle to take suggestions or leadership from others?

Has something happened in my past or childhood that has made me resistant to authority?

Has someone in my past abused their position and taken advantage of me?

Do I have trust issues around those in authority?

Am I fearful that anyone in authority may hurt me?

If you are rebelling against authority because of something that has happened in your past, you could be hindering your healing and your future spouse will have to pay the price. Male or female, during marriage, you will be required to follow some kind of instruction – even if the instruction is given gently, it is still a request for action. If your wife asks you to turn off the light before you come to bed, it is a request for action. If your husband asks you to meet him in the car park as you are both running late, it is a request for action.

Before you enter into marriage, consider whether there is anyone from your past that abused their authority over you that you need to forgive.

There are those that consider themselves to be above instruction. I know someone who feels insulted and undermined if his spouse suggests that they use the Sat Nav when he is driving. He wants to be trusted by his wife and finds it insulting and infuriating if she questions his right turn. I asked him if he did ever take wrong turns. His answer was, 'That's not the point! She should trust me to get her there without questioning me!' Mmmmm! Marriage is partnership. God gives both parties gifts and qualities that will empower and strengthen the marriage. Dictatorship has no place in a successful marriage. This type of person should consider whether he/she wants to sit on a throne and reign from above while his/her subjects follow their every command. They may get some fulfilment from being in charge but as no-one is deemed good enough to be alongside them – it could turn out to be a very lonely life indeed.

Time

We lead busy lives. Do you have the time to commit to a relationship? This may seem like a bizarre question, but anyone who has been in a relationship will tell you that it is all consuming. Even if you are in a relationship where you don't necessarily see each other very often, your thoughts and emotions are caught up with this person. Then add the messaging and phone calls – it all takes up a considerable amount of time. If you are able to spend time together regularly, there is a lot of time spent hanging out, travelling from place to place, visiting friends and family and attending special occasions together.

Even when the relationships aren't going so well, there is a lot of time spent arguing, crying, waiting, wondering, healing etc.

It all takes *TIME!*

If you desire to be in a relationship, you must make time to nurture it and assist in its growth and development. Your relationship cannot slot in after everything else you have going on. It must be given due attention. Of course, finding a balance is important here. It is not realistic to not give time to a relationship, but it is also unwise to abandon other commitments to be together all the time.

Rob and I saw each other almost every day when we were dating. Our 'courtship' was short, and we married after 11 months of dating, but we packed a lot into our courtship. We both attended the same church and we were involved in some of the same ministries within the church, so that allowed us to see each other often. On the days when we were not ministering or serving together we would make our meeting brief but meaningful. For example, during the time that we were dating, I was running a small group for young women at our church on a Thursday evening. On a number of occasions, I would pull over in the local car park and exit my car. Rob would be there waiting. He would come over to me, wrap his arms around me and give me a big squeeze. He'd tell me he was going to miss me that evening and off he would go. My love tank would be filled to overflowing as I made my way to my session with the young ladies. Some days I thought I would burst. We would then speak later on after the session on my way home – sometimes into the early hours. My love tank was filled to overflowing but my sleep tank was often close to empty.

A wonderful young man whom we have adopted into our family once entered into a relationship at a period of time when he was working two jobs, study for a degree and serving in, not one, but two ministries within our church. In a very short space of time he realized that he really did not have the time required to undertake a successful relationship. He had had no idea about the demands of a relationship and once it was over he made the decision to remain single until he was able to give more commitment and time to the next one. A wise young man!

Are you an asset?

Asset - a useful and desirable thing or quality.

Would this describe you? Would you be an asset to another person? Having spent time with you would that person think of you with joy or with dread? Are you pleasant to be around? Optimistic, encouraging, helpful, caring, honest, loving, thoughtful, selfless, understanding, flexible, generous, friendly, kind, fun loving, compassionate, empathetic, patient?

Or are you grumpy, moany, whingy, negative, gossipy, selfish, judgmental, pessimistic, cold, narrow-minded, rigid, unfriendly, boring, thoughtless, unsympathetic and rude.

Honestly, most of us are a combination of both but I certainly strive to be more like the first list.

If you find yourself saying things like:

'That's just the way I am. He/she can take it or leave it!'

'They will just have to fit into my world. I've worked too long and hard to get where I am today to change the way I am now.'

'I'm not prepared to change my whole

life to accommodate someone else when I'm not even sure they are going to stick around!'

'I am no-one's cook and cleaner. He had better come prepared to share the load equally. I have a career too.'

If any of these statements sound familiar, maybe you might want to consider why potential dates don't stick around. These are the mind-sets of people who want to be in relationships or marriage for what they can get out of it. Whether it's sex, cooked meals, companionship, status, culture, children, tax benefits or a clean home, these types of people are not desiring a partnership that produces the best for both parties – and glory for God.

If your relationship is giving you more headache than humor and more pain than pleasure, consider whether you are prepared to live with that pain and headache for the rest of your lives together. Of course, this is a decision to be made before marriage. Once you say, 'I do', you are in it for life. If you are marrying someone with a mind-set that you can get out (divorce) if it gets difficult, please, for everyone's sake, walk away now, before you sign that marriage certificate.

Most of us do not intend to hurt others or act selfishly. Pain from previous relationships are a major factor when entering into a new relationship. We proceed with caution and we have our guard up. And, this is fine. In fact, this is wise. Who would get burnt, escape, and then walk straight back into the fire again? We move forward with caution and check to see if there are flames. For sure. But, some of us move forward with caution holding a flaming torchlight. You know the torches that were used historically made up of a wooden stick with a rag soaked in pitch wrapped around one end? We meet someone new and we have the torch blazing away at arm's length in front of us, warning the person that we have a weapon and we are not afraid to use it. Meanwhile, that person arrives home after a date with us with a burnt nose and eyebrows scorching, wondering what on earth they did to deserve all the fire that just came at them. Sound familiar?

Let's make time to deal with our hurts before we

inflict that hurt on others. Healing and forgiveness can take time to process and sink in. (More on this later).

Have you ever been in the company of someone who seems to do nothing but see the negative in everything? I'm talking about those people for whom the sun setting is an issue. You could be sitting on a river bank, watching the sun slowly descending, its beautiful colors setting the water ablaze with yellows, oranges and stunning shades of red. And somehow, that person can only think about the fact that it will probably turn cold soon, seeing as the sun has gone down and they are scrambling to their feet to head off to the nearest station. Again, these characters drain me – they literally drain my joy. One hour with them is torturous. Being married to someone like that is not worth thinking about.

I remember a couple we encountered a few years ago. She was bright and bubbly and high-pitched. She lived her life zipping from one task to another, packing everything in and was generally upbeat and fast-paced. He was structured and organized, always on time and far more serious about life in general. She would throw her head back and laugh out loud, he would smile and nod in appreciation of the joke. She would dance in the street if she heard a song she loved. He would take out his phone, identify the song and make a note of it to play later in his private setting. She would call him pet names and 'baby' him a little. He wished she would grow up and take life more seriously. They were talking about marriage. I met with them separately and helped them to understand that they were draining each other. Neither of them could really be themselves, their true selves, when they were together. They couldn't see it, but they were sucking the life out of each other and were heading for a life of misery. Thankfully, they made the very wise decision to part ways.

Being with someone who you cannot be yourself with will eventually drain you. You will lose yourself and suppress much of what is natural to you. Eventually resentment will set in and you will no longer be able to identify the real you.

Question: Do you know the real you?

No?

Singleness is a great way to find *you*. Who you are, what you like, what you don't like etc. And, who better to ask about you than the One who created you. Find yourself in Him *then* find the one who will compliment you.

So, having looked at these twelve categories of the self-analysis, and having considered the answers to some of the questions, the question I have to ask is; Would you date *YOU*?

If you went on a date with yourself would you arrange a second date?

Remember, we are all a work in progress and none of us are perfect – not even close. But are there some things you feel the need to work on before you attach yourself to someone else?

Have a look at the list below and make a note of anything you think you need to address. (If you have a close, trusted friend or family member that you could ask to give some feedback on their analysis of you, feel free to do this. Just be prepared to hear some feedback that may take you by surprise).

Christian?

_____

_____

_____

_____

_____

_____

Studying the Word?

_____

_____

_____

_____

_____

_____

Fruits of the Spirit?

_____

_____

_____

_____

_____

_____

Prayer?

_____

_____

_____

_____

_____

_____

Good Steward?

_____

_____

_____

_____

_____

_____

_____

Serving?

_____

_____

_____

_____

_____

_____

Appearance?

_____

_____

_____

_____

_____

Attitude?

_____

_____

_____

_____

_____

_____

_____

Submissive?

_____

_____

_____

_____

_____

Under Authority?

_____

_____

_____

_____

_____

_____

Time?

_____

_____

_____

_____

_____

_____

Are you an Asset?

_____

_____

_____

_____

_____

_____

Singleness

I'd like to take a moment to address the *'elephant in the room'*. I have heard so many alternative words and phrases for the word 'single'. There are some people that do not want to be called *single*. They do not want that label. They do not want to be identified as one of *those* people. In some arenas, the word single seems to hold the same connotation as the word leper. It is certainly not a word that can be used freely in the church setting, for fear of ostracizing an individual or group of individuals that would fit into that category. It is almost as if there is an imaginary cage to the far side and/or rear of the building that contains these strange specimens and every so often (not often enough, as far as the captured are concerned) one manages to break free and joins the prestigious group called the 'marrieds' whom are free to roam wherever they choose and integrate with the accepted elite of society.

The single people may see it that way and many have told me that that is exactly what it feels like for them. 'Married' is the end goal for a high percentage of single people and beyond a certain age, the question arises, 'What is wrong with me?'

In my particular case, I was single until I was 32. I came to the Lord at the age of 27 and made a private and personal agreement with God that I did not want to date. I wanted to focus on Him and deal with the multitude of issues that I was carrying with me wherever I went. Five years later, I was wondering whether my deal with God was too far-fetched and had resulted in me 'missing the boat'. I remember my 30th birthday approaching – a 'landmark' in the life of many single women. By that age I had wanted to at least meet the man that I was going to spend the rest of my life with. I planned a private, black-tie dinner party in central London with very close friends and whilst I prepared the seating plan, I strategically left a space beside me for that man. I hadn't met him yet, but I believed God would deliver him. As the planned date drew closer and closer, I still had no name to put on the seating plan or place card. I told myself not to let my faith waiver. 'God can, and will, do it!' I reassured myself.

That evening, dressed in my floor length, black,

evening gown and surrounded by my nearest and dearest friends, I spoke to the person on my right for most of the evening. The chair on my left remained empty. I learned that night that I could not force the hand of God.

As my 30th year passed, followed by my 31st, my plan to meet that man that I was going to share my future with was becoming more of a focus. You see, in my mind, the process of meeting and marrying this guy was a five-year plan. Two years to meet and date, he would then propose. We would be engaged for 18 months whilst I continued to 'test the waters'. All being well, I would then start to plan the wedding, which would take me another 18 months, so, all in all, I had 5 years to make this happen. Once we were married, I planned to spend two years getting to know each other, having all the sex we wanted and travelling the world, finding ourselves. This, of course meant, that we would start having children seven years from the day we met – roughly. So, at 32, by my estimations, taking into account the 9 months of pregnancy, I would be giving birth in my 40's.

You can imagine, I was starting to get a little impatient with all the waiting. Now, I use the word impatient because I was wanting this plan to happen sooner rather than later, but I was not desperate or foolish. There were a few men along the way that decided I was to be their wife. One in particular, beat his fist against my front door early one morning. As I opened the door, bleary eyed and more than a little bit frustrated, he declares that he had a dream and God told him I was to be his wife. (We weren't even dating). My stomach turned. Maybe I was still dreaming – or having a nightmare. I could think of nothing worse. I mean, he was a nice enough guy, but he did nothing for me. Mentally, physically, spiritually – there was nothing. Not from my direction anyway. He was a Christian, he was handsome, he was intelligent, he was polite, he was cultured, he presented himself very well, but, there was no connection for me. Above all, whilst he was telling me that God had told him that I was his wife, God wasn't telling me anything. And, until I hear God's voice telling me or confirming anything, it's a no-go for me.

During this period, I had been praying and fasting

for my husband who was to come. This, for me, was not a random act instigated by self, not at all. A couple of years prior, whilst I was a part of my church worship team, we had recorded an album in a recording studio in Portsmouth. During the recording, whilst we were experiencing some unplanned free worship, the presence of the Holy Spirit was felt so strongly, it was almost tangible. The following day, back at our home church, a dear auntie who was also a member of the worship team came and told me that, following the experience the previous day, the Lord had laid on her heart to pray and fast with me concerning my future helpmate. It caught me by surprise, but I agreed, and we began the process of praying and fasting on the 20th of each month.

What I discovered throughout this time of preparation is that distractions will come to throw you off of the original plan – God's plan. I truly believe that if it wasn't for two things; my fear of marrying the wrong person and living in torment and my dependence and direction from God, I could now be married to any one of those guys who had offered me a future.

I continued to pray and fast and, through Christ I began to know my husband, even though he hadn't yet arrived. I know! Bizarre, right? But, in all honesty, during my many prayer sessions I felt as if I knew him. There was a time that I was praying in tongues and my prayers became urgent. My tone changed, my physical stance became soldier-like. My fists were clenched. I felt like I was fighting for my life – or someone's life. I was in warfare. I didn't know what was happening, but I knew it was on my shoulders to fight and win. I sensed it was something to do with my future husband and as I was coming to the end of my prayer time, but still feeling fired up, my language changed back to English and I remember saying something along the lines of, *'Lord, I command anything and anyone that stands in the way of me receiving my blessing from you to be torn down and removed, in the name of Jesus. I claim what is rightfully mine and I cast out any distraction, disruption or harm that is being placed between us.'* As I said these words, I felt a sense of calm and peace. I also felt that I was fulfilling an assignment that had been given to me and that I was somewhat responsible for. I was being positioned as a prayer warrior for this cause and I couldn't sleep on the job. During that stage of my life I lived alone and had plenty of time to spend with God - in His word and in prayer. I also spent a lot of time in silence, just listening for His next instruction. I loved it. No, I LOVED it! I would go as far as to say that I became very selfish about God. I felt He was mine and mine alone and I wanted more and more of Him. My communication with Him felt so phenomenal – I wanted nothing else. I will add here that although I was enjoying my time with God, I would often feel intense loneliness. My desire for someone to share my life with was increasing by the day and there were days when I could almost taste it, and then there were days that it all felt so distant and impossible. I always felt it would happen someday, but it always felt as though it was just out of arms reach. As much as I wanted to be married with children, a part of me couldn't quite picture it. That picture had no frame of reference.

Towards the end of my three years of praying and fasting, I was invited to our annual Church Weekend Away. (I won't go into too much detail here as I have already covered this in my first book but, in case you haven't read it….) An older lady who was a part of the worship team invited me to attend. I wasn't planning to go and, at first, I declined the invitation. That night, the invitation wouldn't leave my mind and the following day I asked if the offer was still available. It was, and I went. The second evening there Rob popped his head round the door of the room I was sitting in and I beckoned him over. We had not spoken before, but I had seen him around church on Sundays. I knew his name but not much more. As he came over, looking curious and a little apprehensive, I said to him, 'I need to find you a wife.'

To this day, I do not know why I said that. I can tell you now, I was not thinking that it would be me. But God, knew, and this was how He chose for us to meet.

Within two weeks we knew that we were to be husband and wife and within 11 months we were married. May I take this opportunity to remind you about my five-year plan! Well, God had another plan. I was married at 32 and we had our first son when I was 35.

Singleness, for me, was a time of preparation. Not preparation for the person I was to marry, although he would, of course, benefit. No, it was a time for me to discover who I was. Not the person I had become having been through many hurts and disappointments. Not the person the world was dictating I should be, i.e. an independent, strong woman who was equal to and no less than any man. Not the person who was fearful of failure and poverty. Not the person who was blowing along in the wind hoping to land on a pretty perch and not some dried-out animal dung. This discovery of self was about finding out who the Almighty Creator of all things had created me to be. I was intrigued to find out who or what I was like without all the 'stuff'. The stuff that had made me angry or fearful or cautious or bitter or selfish. The stuff that may have made me stronger but had also made me less effective and more defensive. The stuff that had caused me to build a barrier of protection around myself, and that protection was refusing to let *anyone* in. In fact, I was no longer letting myself out. I had separated myself from life – only coming out with a mask on, dragging along heavy armor. I wanted to know who the real Sonia was and whilst I could enquire of those who knew me, they only really knew the me I allowed them to see. God, on the other hand, knew the real Sonia. The one He had created and chosen. The one with whom the scars did not show, and the hurts were external. He knew my inner parts. The parts the scars hadn't reached. The parts that could only be seen by Him. *I* didn't even know them. I could only turn to Him for the truth and I had learnt that the truth was in Him.

As you will discover in the next chapter, *Roots & Fruit*, the deeper parts of any person are always hidden away. Whether it is intentional or not, we do not display our true selves for all to see. Many of us go through life either masking the real person or not digging any deeper to find out who that real person is. We roll along, following the pattern of 'life'. Without the distraction of others (husband and children), singleness allowed me to discover God and the truth about *Sonia* (a continuous journey).

Rob's story of singleness:

Prior to becoming a Christian at the age of 24 I had been in relationships that had resulted in regret and frustration. These relationships did not end well.

My new-found faith was life changing and I had renewed hope in being able to conduct relationships positively. I was under no illusion that, in all of my past relationships, whether long term or short, I was usually the common denominator for them not working out.

As a young boy, growing up in an all-female environment, despite having all the inside knowledge on what made women tick and the insight into what they talk about or say about men, I actually lacked confidence in speaking to females on a romantic level. This lack of confidence stemmed from not wanting to be rejected. The embarrassment that I would feel if any advances were rebuffed was enough to stop me making my *move*.

Later into my teens, my confidence increased, and I had come into my own. Using my sense of humor and lessons learnt from female friends I learned how to navigate the extreme vortex of females and relationships.

There is a song that says, 'The first cut is the deepest', (Marcia Griffiths).

How true this is. I relate this to, what I would describe as, (I can't believe I am actually writing this down) my first love! Well, that's how I would have described my feelings at the time. This was my first 'girlfriend' that I actually really did like. Let's keep it at that. You know what I'm trying to say. Anyway......let's just say, from my perspective, it didn't end too well. She more or less dumped me. Yeah, something like that. I remember that she didn't do it in a nasty way or try to embarrass me, but although I held it up when we were face to face and walked away with my pride intact, I went home and was a bit..... 'emotional' – let's put it that way, to the point where my mum would come into my room to see if I was okay.

Let me make it clear - I was not in bits or crying into my pillow or anything, I just wasn't my usual bubbly self. It was at this point that I said to myself, 'I will NEVER give another female the power to make me feel this way again!!!'

There began the process of broken relationship after broken relationship - which left a trail of destruction. It was not intentional though.

I believe that the rest of my relationships, after this point, were shaped by a subconscious shield around my heart triggered by emotions stemming from that 'first cut' as a teenager.

Coming into a church environment was a totally different and yet a familiar place for me. Again, it was a female dominated place. Well, in the sense of sheer numbers. I found myself in a place where I was comfortable, and this led to the challenges of inappropriate communication and lack of boundaries with regards to the females I came into contact with.

I think this is a good place to state that, with regards to relationships within the church, there were no situations that required church discipline to an alarming level. However, I do recall being invited into pastor Steve's office after a Sunday evening service for a conversation about my conduct with females within the church. Pastor Steve explained that my behavior could lead to problematic scenario's if I was not careful. I also remember Pastor Steve speaking and treating me like a son. I declared, right there and then that I would not be speaking to any girls going forward. Pastor Steve, with a little smile on his face said, 'Well, I wouldn't go that far. But, just consider the impact of your words and the time you spend with females.' That was all that I needed for the message to come through loud and clear. He spoke to me with love, not conviction. It was that conversation and the mild rebuke that changed something within me – well, in church anyway.

Outside of church, I continued to struggle with the opposite sex. The first two years of my Christian walk could easily have been coined by the phrase '1 step forward, 2 steps back'. Let's leave that one there……..

Towards the end of those two years I arrived at a place of despair. I desired 'the' relationship and, dare I say, 'Marriage' which seemed to be the topic on everyone's lips. Here I was, desperately in love with God, having experienced the transforming power of Jesus in my life, but on the other hand, I was still entrenched in a culture and lifestyle that was at odds with what I now believed. Torn by my personal struggles with relationships and the opposite sex, and after coming out of a very emotional place of yet another broken friendship/relationship, I had had enough!

In the midst of this experience I lost my mum. Although she was not a picture of health, this loss come totally out of the blue. One minute she was here, the next she was gone. Emotionally I was a mixed bag. Strong, but also weak.

The loss of my mum numbed me and pushed me deeper into a relationship that was already heading in the wrong direction. On reflection, the grieving process was somehow justifying the comfort I received from engaging emotionally in the relationship - in a strange and somewhat twisted way. I did not want to feel the guilt of causing pain to another person in my life, especially now that I was a Christian and trying to live right.

The guilt and self-condemnation overwhelmed me AGAIN. I got very serious with God and declared, 'That's it! I'M DONE with this whole relationship thing!' Despite having said a similar thing in THAT conversation with Pastor Steve, this time was different. For possibly the first time, I could see the impact of my involvement with another life and the negative and destructive influence I was having on them.

I wanted out of the relationship. It wasn't good for me or for her. But I had to 'man up' and realize what I was doing, not only to myself but to others.

Something took place within me and I declared to God, 'It's just You and me now. This girl *ting* is not working out for me!'

Over the following week, I was very focused, but I still had to deal (emotionally) with the consequences of my previous actions. It was very difficult - trying to explain something that I did not fully understand myself. All I knew was that a decision had been made and there was no going back or negotiations to be had on the subject. However, I still had to deal with things in a sensitive manner.

During this process the Church Weekend Away was approaching and I was looking forward to it, more so as an escape from the reality of my current situation. I was maintaining my new regime of me and God and I could feel the transformation already, but, based on my previous track record I was concerned that it would not be too long before those two backward steps came into play.

They never did......

That same weekend in November 2003 I engaged in another life changing relationship.

But this one was different.

And, as with all great endings, the rest is history.

Both Rob and I had different experiences of single life – especially as Christians but both were essential to our growth and development as individuals.

Singleness is an essential time in the life of each one of us. Being single is not a *problem* or an *illness* that needs to be cured! Remember, God did not begin the human family with a couple. He began with ONE! In Genesis, God created man first and gave him a lot to do before the woman was even created. The woman was then created for a purpose; to be the helper to the man. Having created the woman, the word then explains that the man will leave his father and mother and unite with his wife and become one flesh. They were not created at the same time. In Adam's singleness he had much to do and fulfil.

Pros and Cons of being Single

Take this opportunity to jot down your feelings around being single. Writing down your thoughts will give you a chance to reflect on where you are right now. This list may change depending on the stage of life you are at currently. Singleness in your teens and twenties may feel different to singleness in your forties and fifties. Try to dig deep and complete both sides of the list.

PRO'S	CON'S

Marriage

God knows the end from the beginning. He knows the end result for each of us and He patiently walks us through the stages of life to get us there.

91

When we have a vision for our marriage, our singleness and dating take on new meaning.

Many of us enter into marriage and *hope* it will be good. How many of us enter into marriage with a vision or goal for what our marriage will be like? I'm not talking about the airy-fairy childlike dreams of being married with two point four children (a boy and a girl), a cute, fluffy dog and a white picket fence surrounding a gingerbread cottage. No. I'm talking about legacy, impact, calling, purpose etc. What example will you be to others? What example will you give your children to follow. What impact will you leave on others. What difference will you make to the world around you? What will you be remembered for? How will your contribution build up God's kingdom on earth?

When you have a vision for your marriage you can begin to prepare yourself and set the foundation during your singleness. But how, I hear you ask. Let me give you an example.

So, you are a young man who has continuously struggled to retain or save money. Whatever you earn is spent within the month. As the next pay day approaches, you find yourself with the last few pounds in your wallet and your bank balance is £500 *in debit*. That overdraft is not reducing over time despite your promises to yourself that you would have it paid off over 6 months. Your parents always struggled to retain money and they lived with a very similar financial pattern to you. You have enough money to live on and if you set your mind to it you could potentially save at least £400 per month. However, you consider yourself to be someone who likes to present himself well – and you don't mind spending that little bit extra to get the best quality. So, every month you buy yourself something new – just to keep up with the trends of the season. You also enjoy eating out and you like to spoil the children in your life – your exceptionally cute niece who melts your heart every time you see her and your Godson who is fast becoming a little mini-me of you. Whilst there is nothing wrong with any of the above there is a part of you that would like to make more of an impact than just looking good, eating well and treating others occasionally.

You begin to search deeper and you ask God how He would want to use you. You question your reason and purpose for being in this world at this time. You would like to make an impact in some way.

Now, consider a couple of things; if you were to marry someone who was just like you with regards to their spending habits, you would both understand each other's desire to spend but you would both be spending excessive money and leaving no impact. If you continued spending as you are but married someone who was very cautious about money and found your spending to be wasteful, conflict may ensue, and you would now be in a marriage that was turbulent and/or divided.

Your desire to leave an impact gains momentum in your heart and in your mind and you begin to feel that you could do more with your money. You have a desire to invest in something more than nice clothing and fine dining. You have always wanted to play a part in helping the young people in your community to have access to further education. What if you could fund places for university courses – even for just one young person!

Could this be your vision? Could it be even bigger than this?

With this in mind you could set some imminent goals – pay off the overdraft in 3 months, limit yourself to new clothing once every two to three months, buy your Godson some sweets instead of Prada trainers and eat home-cooked food instead of eating out so often.

As your *single* mindset changes, your *marriage* mindset also begins to change. As a single person, you now have something to aspire to, a goal to work towards, a vision to aspire to. Do you choose to marry someone who aligns with that vision? Or do you choose to marry someone who wants to spend, spend, spend on Jimmy Choo's? Bear in mind, your vision doesn't have to be her vision – she may have a different vision, but, does she have any vision? Or, is she blowing in the wind? If your vision for marriage is to be effective, purposeful and intentional, do you marry someone who is frivolous, flighty and thoughtless. If you are caring, calm and cautious, do you marry someone who is careless, irresponsible and argumentative?

Your vision can be based on how effective you wish to be as a couple and/or how you envisage your home and family life. Either way, don't leave it to chance. Use your singleness to set the foundation and begin to prepare for what is to come.

2

ROOTS & FRUIT

When we meet someone for the first time we have no idea of what is sitting under the surface. The roots of any person are well hidden but just like plants and trees, you may occasionally see the odd root appearing from below the surface. Usually this takes place with either; older or well-established plants/trees or this tends to happen when a plant needs re-potting. As humans, we tend to observe things from the surface level and above. This is natural. The visual appearance tends to be the first thing we notice if we meet someone in person. If the 'meeting' is verbal, i.e. via a phone call we take more notice of the way someone sounds. If we do not have the opportunity or ability to see or hear, we tend to go with touch, or smell – our other senses kick in. However, none of these allow us to see, hear, touch, smell, what is under the surface. As we get to know someone and spend more time with them, our roots will begin to surface over time – but there are some roots we would rather keep below the surface, keep hidden, keep private.

When I was 13 years old, I went on holiday with my mum and sister. My parents were divorced, and my sister and I would visit my Dad on Sundays, every week. As my sister got older, she made the decision to no longer visit my Dad, but I wasn't old enough to make that decision for myself, so I continued to visit every week. On return from my holiday I went to visit my Dad as usual, but this occasion was different.

My Dad was very angry with me and at first, I couldn't fathom what was happening. As far as I was aware I hadn't done anything to make him angry, but he was furious with me. He was shouting at me and he told me to get my things together because he was taking me home. I did as he instructed and when we pulled up outside my home having driven in silence my Dad said to me,

"I'll see you when I see you. And, if anyone asks you who your Dad is, tell them you haven't got one." He stopped talking, I stepped out of the car and he pulled away. That was the last I saw of him for seventeen years.

On the surface I looked the same. But my roots had changed. Of course, they had grown but the story they would tell if they were asked would be a very different story than if I had not had that encounter with my Dad. Each root had a label; some were labelled with positive, encouraging, edifying words whilst others were labelled with words like; rejection, anger, frustration, shame, blame, low self-esteem, embarrassment, bitterness, pride. These labels were being formed by what was happening to me, not what I was *choosing* to happen to me.

My impression of relationships was being formed based on what I was seeing around me – and it wasn't positive. It was around that time, at the age of thirteen, that I began to build my wall of protection around me. My wall had many, many layers - just in case someone tried to penetrate one layer I ensured there were several.

At 15, boys started showing an interest in me and although these relationships were purely friendships - just hanging out as groups of friends after school etc. my guard was already up, and I wouldn't allow anyone near my heart. As I got older and began to spend time with guys one to one, I would enjoy their company and we'd be intimate, but my heart was completely and utterly unobtainable. You see, having been rejected by my Dad - the one man in my life that was supposed to love and accept me, no matter what – my thinking was that, any other man was bound to reject me, eventually. I remained in that *safe* place for many, many years.

In many cases, we ourselves do not know or realize what is lurking under the surface. We are not able to identify why we behave a certain way or why particular sounds, smells or sights make us uncomfortable or excited. Some experiences trigger a reaction within us that is unexplainable.

Rob discovered, after a number of years of marriage that a major factor of our conflict was based on the fact that he grew up in an all-female environment with strong female characters. As previously explained, he made a vow as a young man that he would not allow any woman to dominate him or tell him what to do. And then he met me! He didn't always understand why certain words, phrases, my tone of voice or my strong views on a particular subject irritated him. His breakthrough came during a marriage conference that we attended together. The keynote speaker touched on a particular subject and Rob was transported back to his past. He turned to me and with wonder and revelation written all over his face he explained to me what had just been unearthed. My eyes welled up with tears. They were tears of joy but also tears of relief and diagnosis. I hadn't understood his resistance until that point.

On return from our honeymoon, following a church service, I overheard Rob tell someone that marriage was *hard*. I was horrified! What I received from what Rob had said was that being married to *me* was hard. And, we'd only been married for 2 weeks! I waited until we had left the building - all the time my uneasiness was building. When we got into the car I couldn't hold it in anymore. I asked Rob what he had meant when he said that marriage was hard. He explained that he was finding marriage difficult because he could no longer tuck things away and not deal with them. He went on to explain that, all the 'things' he had buried under the surface, never to be seen again, were resurfacing – and he didn't like it. I was probing and asking questions in my attempt to get to know him and he couldn't escape, the way he would have done in his past. (More on this later).

Both Rob and I have roots that tell a story – mostly stories that we don't want to tell, but relationships will bring roots to the surface and who knows what happens when roots become exposed and are at risk of damage? What happens to the tree or plant?

Stay with me.

Ever wondered why we see lots of worms when there has been heavy rainfall? Well, the quick answer is that the worm burrows fill with water and also the worms can't get enough oxygen when soil is flooded so they come to the surface to breathe. In society, we often describe difficult times as rainy days. Christians often use this phrase, 'When the rains come...' We associate rain, especially heavy, prolonged rain with difficult times. We are well aware of the benefits of rain and yet we tend to see it as a negative. Much like worms, when we encounter difficult times (rain), certain behaviors rise to the surface but also, the 'rain' can trigger emotions that we have buried.

Another factor to consider when it comes to our buried secrets is the role of the gardener. Just as a gardener will cultivate, dig and rake his soil, there will be people who will come into our lives and start digging and raking through our private thoughts, fears and secrets. The gardener will do what he does to get the best from his soil. But imagine if the soil had feelings. The gardener would be causing pain and discomfort to the soil. Well, we *do* have feelings. And someone digging around and raking through our past can hurt. It would certainly feel uncomfortable. But, now consider the outcome for the soil. Having been raked and dug and cultivated it would be ready for planting and growing and nourishing. *Who* is doing the digging can determine the level of discomfort. For example, a counsellor will dig into our past but as we are most likely meeting with the counsellor having agreed to have counselling sessions, the *digging* is expected. This may still feel uncomfortable, but at least it is expected. When a stranger or somebody that you do not know very well starts to *dig*, it can come as a surprise or shock and you may very quickly recoil and hide.

When we enter into new relationships, to begin with, that person is a stranger. Yet, one of the first things we do is ask questions, particularly about their past, or their family, or their education, or their childhood experiences. Any one of these categories could *rake* up feelings of hurt or shame or disappointment, and yet, dating gives us unspoken permission to go there. When this happens our 'roots' become exposed and we can feel vulnerable, angry, worried or maybe excited!

Take some time to consider the following questions:

When do you feel most vulnerable?

_____

_____

_____

_____

_____

What am I like when I'm angry?

_____

_____

_____

_____

_____

What am I like when I'm worried?

_____

_____

_____

_____

What am I like when I'm excited?

The answers to these questions will help you to understand what may be lingering under the surface. Knowing what *makes* you angry or worried may help you to consider what *causes* the anger or worry and in turn may help you to identify the root of the anger or worry.

If a child has experienced abandonment they may grow up to worry that they may be abandoned by others. This worry may seem irrational to some but logical to that child who is now an adult. That same adult may get angry when they arrange to meet someone at a set time and the person is 30 minutes late. The person who is late may feel that the adult is being irrational – 30 mins isn't that long, after all, is it? Well, to the person who has experienced abandonment, the focus isn't the length of time, the focus is the absence of the person. You may say, well, why doesn't the adult just explain to people why they don't like people to be late? Well, that would make them vulnerable. We don't like to feel vulnerable, do we? Vulnerability can feel like weakness or exposure. So, we tend to try and keep these feelings deep down below the surface so that we do not have to deal with them. But relationships and marriage stir them up repeatedly.

 Are you ready to let the gardener in?

In an ideal world, the fruit that we display should be indicative of the roots that lie below. Juicy, healthy fruit should tell us that all is well beneath the surface, right? Well, remember in the previous chapter, we spoke about the fruits of the spirit. That's the kind of fruit we want to see on that tree! We often display a smiling face, nice clothes, beautiful hairstyles, perfectly cropped goatees and beards and jewelry but those things can be changed and/or removed.

✏️ Remind yourself of the **FRUITS OF THE SPIRIT** *(complete the grid below):*

💭 Ask yourself, am I displaying the fruits of the spirit as I go about my day?

I mentioned earlier about exposed roots. Should we expose our roots and bring them above the surface for all to see? The short answer is, no! We should not allow ourselves to be exposed and trampled on. This will inevitably cause damage, or harm, or hurt.

'Do not give dogs what is sacred – do not throw your pearls to pigs! If you do, they may trample them under their feet and turn and tear you to pieces'.

Matt 7:6 (NIV)

When the roots of a tree are damaged beyond repair the tree begins the process of dying. This process can take a long time to happen. The tree will appear to still have life in it, and although changes will appear above the surface, those changes will be accepted as the naturally occurring aging process. The same can happen with us. On the surface we can seem fine, we still smile, we still function as we have done but inside we are dying away. There are a number of factors that cause this but neglect, harm and the wrong environment are the main factors. Instead we should gain understanding and deal with our fears, hurts, anger, bitterness and unforgiveness before we invite someone else to join with us, for if neither party deals with these underlying issues before entering into a relationship or marriage, there are sure to be emotional problems ahead. As with a dying plant, good soil, water and sunlight will aid the process of healing and restoration. In our case, being planted in the right environment (soil), gaining knowledge and understanding (water) and being nourished from within (sun) will give the right environment to heal and grow. As Christians, our soil is church, our water is The Word and our sun is the Holy Spirit.

Residing with Christ is the nourishment we need to be made whole. In singleness, this process is made easier. I'm not saying it's an easy process, I'm saying it's easier without the distractions of marriage. Without the distractions of marriage, we can rest in Christ, focus on what He has to say and allow His love to penetrate. Of course, this is all a process and we all heal and recover at a different pace and so, we have to give ourselves, and each other, time to heal and repair.

"I am the true grapevine, and my Father is the gardener. He cuts off every branch of mine that doesn't produce fruit, and he prunes the branches that do bear fruit so they will produce even more. You have already been pruned and purified by the message I have given you. Remain in me, and I will remain in you. For a branch cannot produce fruit if it is severed from the vine, and you cannot be fruitful unless you remain in me. Yes, I am the vine; you are

the branches. Those who remain in me, and I in them, will produce much fruit. For apart from me you can do nothing. Anyone who does not remain in me is thrown away like a useless branch and withers. Such branches are gathered into a pile to be burned. But if you remain in me and my words remain in you, you may ask for anything you want, and it will be granted! When you produce much fruit, you are my true disciples. This brings great glory to my Father.

John 15:1–8 (NLT)

What would help **YOU** to move on from hurt or unforgiveness? (i.e. a conversation, an apology, a confession etc.)

_____

_____

_____

_____

Be honest with yourself. Does anyone come to mind as you ask yourself that question? Ask God to reveal to you any person that has hurt or offended you in your past. Do not be fearful of allowing your mind to go back there. However, if the very thought of that person (or situation) causes you so much pain that you are fearful about recalling memories of them, I strongly advise that you seek professional help. If you will not consider professional help, please allow me to suggest what your future may look like.

In my personal experience, I lived with *anger* (at my dad), *frustration* (at not being able to explain myself to my Dad), *fear* (initially, that someone else would hurt me the same way - but also that I would bump into my dad and not know what to say), *denial* (that what my dad said to me was having an effect on my life), *rejection* (because he was supposed to love me – no matter what), *bitterness* (that I couldn't be who I really wanted to be – just in case someone took advantage of my kind nature and mistreated me), *regret* (that I hadn't tried to speak up and explain at the time), *guilt* (that deep down, despite what had happened, I was glad I didn't have to visit my dad every Sunday). Until I truly forgave my dad, those emotions travelled with me every day. Awake or asleep, I was bound by these feelings' day in and day out. Eventually, it became easier to shut myself away – sometimes physically but mostly emotionally and mentally. I built my wall of defense higher and higher and thickened the walls regularly so that no more harm could come to me. But, in my attempt to keep others out, *I* was no longer able to get out! I was losing myself – more importantly, I was losing purpose. I was good for nothing – or so the enemy would have me think. Meanwhile, as far as I was aware, my dad was living his life. I didn't give it much thought because I didn't like to think about it. It hurt too much.

It could also be the case that, the person that as hurt you doesn't even know that they have hurt you. Or they may not know the severity of the hurt. My point is, as long as you remain in a position of unforgiveness you are set to remain imprisoned and ineffective. Those who love you, do not want this for you - but are you able to identify that you do not want this for yourself.

What/who do you think people 'see' when they meet you or enter into any kind of relationship with you? *(It may be useful to ask someone who knows you very well to give you some feedback on their interaction with you).*

_____

_____

_____

_____

_____

_____

_____

_____

_____

Painting courtesy of Helen Yousaf

Is there a part of you that is intent on revenge towards those have hurt you?

> *Dear friends, never take revenge.*
> *Leave that to the righteous anger of God.*
> *For the Scriptures say, "I will take revenge;*
> *I will pay them back," says the Lord.*
> **Romans 12:19 (NLT)**

How can I move on?

There are many, many quotes about forgiveness. Here are a few that I found particularly helpful along my own journey of forgiveness;

> 'Unforgiveness is like sipping poison each day and expecting the other person to die.'

> 'Unforgiveness doesn't hurt the one who you refuse to forgive – they couldn't care less. Unforgiveness hurts the one who refuses to forgive, and the bitterness grows like a cancer making you physically sick. Forgiving is a choice. We must choose to forgive those who hurt us, so that we can heal.'

> Forgiveness doesn't excuse their behavior. Forgiveness prevents their behavior from destroying your heart.'

This last one was the first step for me, in understanding that, to forgive is not to condone their behavior but to free myself from my prison.

If unforgiveness is something you are battling with right now, take it to the Lord in prayer for this is His promise to you:

Then you will call on me and come and pray to me, and I will listen to you. You will seek me and find me when you seek me with all your heart. I will be found by you," declares the LORD, "and will bring you back from captivity.

Jer 29:12-14a (NIV)

Also, seek counselling. I did! It was the best thing I ever did. By the 5th session I was released from the burden I had put upon myself and my approach to pretty much everything was transformed. A word of advice – seek Godly counsel.

Also, be accountable to others – or at least one other. Do not isolate yourself or live in fear, shame or darkness. I have yet to meet someone who doesn't have a story or secret about their past. Whilst it is not advisable to tell all and sundry about your personal battles, it is also unwise to allow that secret to fester and grow until it cripples you. Ask God to reveal to you someone who can be trusted who also has the wisdom and maturity to walk beside you as you emerge from your 'prison' and step into the light.

✎ **I need to forgive.......** *(Insert the name of the individuals that come to mind as you read through this section)*

1.
2.
3.
4.
5.

Did any of your answers above include yourself? Often, we need to forgive ourselves for something we may have said or done that is weighing us down and causing us to feel guilty. Until we release ourselves we remain in that same prison.

Entering in to a relationship, whilst we are still carrying unforgiveness is like inviting that person into your cell with you. They are now imprisoned and serving a sentence for a 'crime' they didn't commit. Do they deserve that? Neither of you deserve that!

🌩 Remember: Christ paid the price for you to be free! Why are you still sitting in the *unlocked* prison cell?

Fallen Fruit

When fruit falls from a tree, a passer-by may pick it up to eat it. Imagine there are two apples sitting at the base of the tree. One is green, shiny, firm and without blemish. The other is brown, soft, wrinkly and bruised. Which one would the passer-by select to eat?

Now, imagine those apples are a reflection of you. Which 'one' would a person chose? The brown, wrinkly, bruised apple is you carrying unforgiveness, locked away in your prison, unable to see or appreciate the sunlight and all the good around you. The green, shiny, firm apple is you, restored, full of hope, expectant and purposeful. Which would you choose?

Consider;

How would you prefer to be seen by others?

When others meet you, do you look like you are carrying the light of Christ and experiencing the joy of the Lord?

Remember, we are made in the image of Christ. We have a responsibility to display Him. Therefore, we should make every effort to replicate and represent Christ.

3
WHO, ME?

'A person's steps are directed by the Lord. How then can anyone understand their own way?

Prov 20:24 (NIV)

The very steps we take come from God; otherwise how would we know where we're going?

Prov 20:24 (MSG)

'Lord, I know that people's lives are not their own; it is not for them to direct their steps.'

Jeremiah 10:23 (NIV)

'For I know the plans I have for you," declares the Lord, "plans to prosper you and not to harm you, plans to give you hope and a future.'

Jeremiah 29:11 (NIV)

Planning for the future

Let's take a look at some of the areas of our lives that require planning;

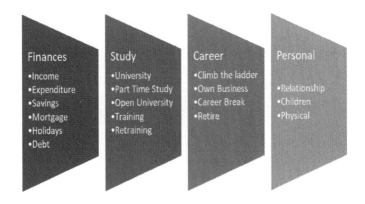

Finances
- Income
- Expenditure
- Savings
- Mortgage
- Holidays
- Debt

Study
- University
- Part Time Study
- Open University
- Training
- Retraining

Career
- Climb the ladder
- Own Business
- Career Break
- Retire

Personal
- Relationship
- Children
- Physical

Different seasons of our lives will require levels of change and adjustment. How do you cope with change? Are you somebody who embraces change and rolls with it? Are you the person that tends to initiate change? Do you tend to resist change but accept that it will come? Or, do you fight, to the very end, kicking and screaming against change with the end result being a boycott or demonstration against the proposed change? Which of these best fits you?

Whether you recognize change as positive or negative, it will come.

Often, change is out of our control. But, remember, God is *always* in control.

With this in mind, ponder on the following question;

💭 Who will you be in 5, 10, 20, 30, 40 years' time?

Consider your answers, but, notice the question says, 'Who will you be?', not, what will you be doing? Often when we are asked a question like this we consider where we will be in our career, how many children we may have, which countries we would have visited, etc. But, I am asking you to consider the person you will be 5, 10, 20, 30, 40 years' from now. It's difficult to know isn't it?

Now consider the person you choose to spend the rest of your life with. Who will *they* be in 5, 10, 20, 30, 40 years' from now? Again, it's difficult to know. It's a gamble.

Both of you, entering into a new relationship, will

be taking a gamble on who you will be in the near and distant future. The bible says:

> *"No eye has seen, no ear has heard, and no mind has imagined what God has prepared for those who love him."*

1 Cor 2:9 (NLT)

This tells me that, no-one but God knows what the future will hold for each of us. Do you agree? In which case, who would be the best person to consult when choosing a partner for life?

Change doesn't just mean seasons of progressing from one stage of life to another. Change also means adjusting your mind, your heart, your thinking and your physical way of doing things to accommodate others. When you initially start to consider dating, you may want to adjust your finances to accommodate additional money that may be spent on meals out, etc. You may want to adjust your appearance if you are not happy with the way you currently look. You may want to adjust your current schedule to make time for dating. My point is, even prior to dating, your mindset will already need to prepare for what is to come.

⬤ Are you prepared to adjust?

The mind is powerful, and it doesn't automatically shift when you are presented with change. Resistance may kick in and you may find yourself resisting even when you thought you were ready for the change.

We will touch more on tolerance in Chapter 4 but for now, let me give you an example of a couple who had to learn to adjust their mindset as they entered into a relationship.

Let's call them Seth and Jenna. Seth had got to a stage in life where he wanted to meet his wife, settle down and have children. Jenna was also ready to do the same. Seth had been independent from a young age and was very capable of taking care of himself. He could cook, wash and clean without assistance and took good care of himself. Seth took his work seriously and was eager to climb the corporate ladder. He worked hard and rarely missed a day of work. Jenna was also independent and could take good care of herself, but she was more of a homemaker. Having a tidy, spotless home was hugely important to her. When they met, Seth and Jenna really enjoyed each other's company and hit it off straight away. Jenna loved Seth's steady, calm, reliable persona and he would make her laugh a lot. She also liked the way he would take charge and make decisions about where they would go on dates etc. Seth loved the way Jenna would banter with him and laugh at his jokes, but he also loved her reliability and inner strength. They both knew they wanted to be together and it didn't take long for them to set their wedding date. Once married, however, Seth began to become frustrated with the way Jenna would constantly clear up after him and fuss over their home. He explained, 'I would come home from work and lay my jacket over the back of the dining room chair whilst I used the bathroom. I'd return to collect my jacket and it would be gone. Jenna would have whipped it up and placed it in the wardrobe before I could blink! She would be the same after dinner. Immediately after eating, I mean, as soon as I had eaten my last forkful, she would jump up, take my plate and whizz it off to the kitchen whilst I was still chewing.' Jenna couldn't understand why Seth would find this frustrating as she saw it as trying to care for him. She was trying her best to be attentive. They both felt awful for trying to do their best but feeling at their worst. They also felt a little ridiculous for meeting with us to complain that she was too tidy! What it really boiled down to, was the fact that Seth didn't want to be treated like an incapable child and Jenna didn't want to feel like an inattentive wife. Both wanted the best for the other one, but they had not discussed what that would look like. Having explained to each of them that adjustment was needed for them to fully understand the needs of the other one, they progressed their relationship without operating on autopilot. Seth adjusted his mindset to that of a married person who no longer needed to care for all his domestic needs as though there was no-one else to care for him. They began to share the household responsibilities and Jenna began to enjoy the opportunities she got to sit and relax whilst Seth made dinner. Jenna adjusted her mindset to help her understand that she didn't need to perform and operate like a Duracell bunny, ensuring everything was perfect and in place at all times to feel that she was a good wife.

Adjusting to what is yet to come seems illogical and somewhat premature but if we do not adjust our minds in the first instance, the challenge comes when you are now in a relationship and you are giving a wrong impression because you may appear selfish, greedy, narrow-minded, possessive or immature – simply because you were not prepared mentally for the shift of thinking of one to thinking of two.

Communication

Communication has been essential since the beginning of time and yet we still struggle with it. When God created the universe, he spoke it into being! God spoke with Adam & Eve in the garden of Eden! And yet, centuries later, we are still failing to communicate clearly, especially in our relationships. There are numerous reasons why we do not communicate what we mean or what we think or what we feel – but, whatever the reason, communication is a primary factor when it comes to relationships.

When Rob and I met we spent a lot of time talking. We saw each other almost every day and we still found time to speak on the phone for hours – it was exhausting. When we attended our pre-marriage course we felt ready for the communication session as we felt we were 'good' in that area. What we discovered was, we were great at talking about our day, what was on TV, what was occurring within our respective families etc. but when it came to talking about ourselves and our feelings and our fears – you get the picture – we were the equivalent of a six-month old baby, just startle to babble, with no real context or subject matter. Into our marriage, our lack of willingness to dig deep and open up about what was under the surface was really highlighted and the volcano that was lying dormant within each of us began to rumble from deep, deep within. The eventual eruption was, as you can imagine, explosive, messy, fiery and it left a lot of scarring.

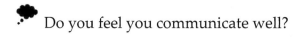 Do you feel you communicate well?

It may be that you speak a lot, or you may be

someone who is more reserved. Or, like Rob and I in our initial stages of our relationship, you are happy to talk, but not about yourself. Are you somebody who tends to remain on the surface when speaking with others, or do you tend to guide the conversation to a deeper level quite quickly? Do you open up to others easily or are you more of a closed book, preferring to keep your private life private? Do you trust easily or are you more suspicious of others?

Let's have a look at a few different levels of communication. Consider where you would place yourself on this diagram:

Let's start at the bottom and work upwards.

Imagine two people at a bus stop. They are there, waiting for a bus. They don't know each other but they are friendly, approachable people with no reason to question or doubt each other. Let's call them Sophie and Michelle.

Surface Level – At this level the level of conversation is as it says, on the surface. No personal details are exchanged, and no specific topic is addressed,

Sophie: Hi.

Michele: Hi.

Conversation has taken place albeit, very brief. Sophie has learnt nothing about Michelle and Michelle has learnt nothing about Sophie. They have been polite, but no connection is made.

More Detail – At this level, information is shared, and facts are being stated.

Sophie: It's warmer today than yesterday huh?

Michelle: Yes, the forecast did say it would be warmer

although I didn't expect it to be this warm. Not for this time of year.

Although Michelle and Sophie are entering in to more depth in their conversation, they are just stating facts about the weather. They are not sharing any information about themselves.

These two levels feel safe for most people. Neither one is digging any deeper and neither one should be feeling vulnerable at this stage.

Deeper Level – Now, we begin to apply some personal detail to the conversation. This can be views on a particular subject or actual experiences.

Sophie: To be honest, I'm not too keen on hot weather.

Michelle: Oh really! Why is that?

Sophie: Well, I'm at that stage of life where I'm getting hot flushes all the time, so the last thing I need is hot weather. It's unbearable.

Sophie has revealed something personal about herself to Michelle and at this point the conversation could go either way. There is some risk involved and Sophie has made herself a little vulnerable by allowing Michelle to know something personal about her. Michelle could decide to shut down the conversation or she could probe for more information by encouraging Sophie. Probing doesn't have to be verbal – it can be body language also. If Michelle were to turn to face Sophie, for example, it would encourage Sophie to continue with what she is saying.

Inclusive – Now we reach a level where feelings become involved.

Michelle: Really! Is it really that bad?

Sophie: Oh, goodness, it's like, the worst feeling and so out of my control. At any point, throughout the day, these burning hot flushes come out of no-where, and there is nothing I can do except remove layers, fan myself franticly and hope it passes quickly. It is so embarrassing when it happens in a meeting at work. I'm sweating everywhere, and everyone can see it, but they don't want to say anything. I hate it!

Michelle: Oh. It's sounds awful.

Sophie: Oh, you have no idea. Just wait until it's your turn love, don't say I didn't warn you!

Sophie has given Michelle an insight into an aspect of her life and told her how she feels about it. Although they don't know each other, Michelle now knows something personal about Sophie and she also knows how it is affecting Sophie's life. At this point Michelle could probe for more information by asking questions and Sophie would probably give her a lot more information. Michelle's interest is encouraging Sophie to open up more – despite not even knowing her.

This level allows the risk and possibility of hurt and pain to come into a relationship because Michelle could use the information to hurt, tease or spread rumors about Sophie.

Intimate – This is the deepest level of conversation. Barriers are lowered, and vulnerability is at its highest level.

Michelle: Well, actually, I'm not sure…. I'm hoping to avoid it.

Sophie: Avoid it! Trust me love, we all have to go through it, us women. It's bad enough what we have to go through having kids, then we have to deal with this. I tell you, men have it easy compared to us.

Michelle: I wouldn't know.

Sophie: Wouldn't know what, love?

Michelle: About having kids.

Sophie: Oh? Have you not had yours yet?

Michelle: I'm not able to. Long story, but I had to have a hysterectomy a few years back and doctors say they are not sure whether I'll experience menopause the way other women do. They said I'd just have to wait and see what happens when I get older.

Sophie: Oh love! I'm so sorry. How insensitive of me. I didn't know........

Michelle has now opened up to Sophie and revealed something she hasn't told many people. Her emotions, feelings and thoughts are all heightened, and she has made herself vulnerable to Sophie.

This level would ordinarily be reserved for the closest person or people to you.

As you can see from the example above, all five levels can be reached in one conversation.

Ordinarily, this depth of conversation would be reserved for your spouse of one or two very close family members or friends, but that would depend on the individual and the circumstances. There are some individuals that will share their most intimate feelings and experiences with all and sundry. This is not advisable for obvious reasons. Wisdom should be used when sharing intimate details with others, but, wisdom is also required when you are sharing intimate information and feelings about yourself or your partner with those that are not (or should not be) in your *intimate* bracket.

As an example, one couple that we mentored were a little confused about 'who should be in what bracket'. She seemed to have a good grasp about where certain friends, colleagues and associates fit into her brackets. He, however, was a little more willing to allow friends into the intimate bracket. He would often spend time with a female work colleague, sharing about his personal struggles, fears, plans etc. He openly admitted that this female was in his intimate bracket. He considered that this was fine seeing as he had been friends with her before his partner had come along. We helped him to understand the dangers of this situation, explaining that his partner, whom he was planning to marry needed to be the closest person to him and that that position should not be shared with anyone else (other than God).

The intimate level brings a level of closeness and privacy that no-one else should be allowed to enter into. He understood in the end!

Complete the communication pyramid on the next page. Insert names (or titles) of family, friends, colleagues etc. Do you have a good balance of people in your life to communicate with?

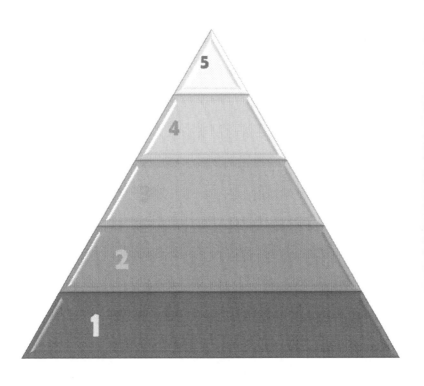

✎ How would you rate yourself as a communicator?

(Poor) 1 2 3 4 5 6 7 8 9 10 (Perfection)

✎ What aspect of communication could you improve on?

_____

_____

_____

Most of us are aware that communication does not just involve talking. Whilst talking is the most obvious aspect of communication it is advisable to recognize that listening is essential during any conversation. And, to be seen to be listening, you also need to respond. Your response can be verbal, with either actual words or encouraging prompts that tell the other person to continue, or that you agree, or disagree. Communication is a two-way process and as you spend time with others you will learn the do's and don'ts of what can help or hinder conversation. We will talk a little more about the do's and don'ts in chapter 6.

Of course, non-verbal communication or body language is a major factor in communicating with others. How we respond with our bodies tells others so much about our level of interest and also our level of comfort. Eye contact, the position of our bodies, our gestures and our general movement will speak volumes when we communicate with others.

I have discovered that I struggle to focus on one thing when there are other things going on around me. So, for example, if I am having a conversation with someone in a restaurant or coffee shop and there are others talking around me, I have to focus intently on listening only to what the person I am with is saying. If I allow myself to zone in to what someone nearby is saying, I totally lose the voice of the person speaking to me. I am the same with my work. I desire absolute silence whilst I work otherwise I get side-tracked. I cannot work with the radio on. I am most productive when there is silence. Also, I have had to train myself, when having conversations with others in public spaces to not look away at what is going on around us. Have you ever had a conversation with someone who keeps looking away at what is going on behind you? Isn't it awful? If or when I am speaking with someone and their eyes are flicking between me and other activity around us, I tend to close the conversation down. I feel that the person clearly isn't interested in what I have to say.

If someone is leaning in, meeting my eye contact, nodding in all the right places and offering me the occasional 'uh-huh' as I speak with them, I generally feel that the conversation is going well. If they ask me to elaborate on something I have said, or they ask questions encouraging me to expand on what I have said, again, I feel the conversation is going well. However, if there are silences, arms are crossed, eyes are flicking around, and fidgeting is going on, conversation is less likely to flow easily, and interest is stunted. Now, of course, consideration needs to be given to those who, for a wide variety of reasons are unable to engage or fit 'the norm' when it comes to social etiquette, but in general, two-way communication is at its best when both parties understand what is required to achieve it.

'Words kill, words give life; they're either poison or fruit—you choose.'

Prov 18:21 (MSG)

'He who guards his mouth preserves his life, But he who opens wide his lips shall have destruction.'

Proverbs 13:3 (NKJV)

In your communication with others, do you lift them up or pull them down with your words? Do you encourage them or discourage them? Are your words poison or fruit?

Do you remember this saying?

'Sticks & stones may break my bones, but names will never hurt me!'

What has your experience been growing up? Have you ever had things said to you that have remained with you to this day? Were they positive words or negative words?

Write those words below and write about how they made you feel. Lastly, write about the effect they have had on your life.

_____

_____

_____

_____

_____

_____

_____

Have you become imprisoned by the negative words that were spoken over you? Are you who you are today because of the encouraging words that were spoken to you.

As explained in Chapter 2 of my first book, as a teenager, my friends (without realizing the impact it would have on me) stated that I would be the first to get married – but I would also be the first to get divorced. They didn't say those words maliciously, with intent to harm – I know that. But, those words had a profound effect on me. For a very long time I believed those words and coupled with the fact that my parents had divorced, I began to plan my future around divorce. As time went on, my plan to marry, divorce and raise my children alone changed.

My new plan was a desire to marry and stay married - but with fear entrenched in the plan. That fear eventually morphed into fight. The fighting will to a) prove my friends wrong, b) follow God's plan, c) have a happy, enjoyable, purposeful marriage, d) offer our children something other than what I had experienced growing up, and e) be an example to those coming up behind us who would be looking for married role models to lead them. For those reasons, I continue to fight.

I have learned that:

'The greatest evangelistic tool is the way you live not what comes out of your mouth!'

Social Media

We are all aware of the popularity of social media in society today. Statistically, at the beginning of 2017, the total number of social media users in the UK had reached over 39 million users, with estimates going up to 42 million users. There is no denying that most of us are using social media in one form or another.

There are many advantages to using social media, from keeping in touch with friends and family to promoting businesses and events. There are those that like to inform others of their every move, from what they had for breakfast to the fact that they are at the airport about to fly out to Cancún. Others prefer to keep their account very private and use it purely to keep in touch with family abroad. For others, promoting and advertising business is the only use they have for social media. Then, of course, there are those who will sit for hours scrolling through pages of their 'friends' accounts – just out of curiosity.

Whatever your use for social media, the fact is, it's here, its huge and it's here to stay.

Of course, like with most things in life, advantages can also have disadvantages, and we should be aware of them. I'd like to make you aware of one of the disadvantages of social media.

When you post a comment or image on social media, the person receiving it may choose to keep it or delete it. They may choose to bypass it or share it. That, of course, is their decision. The receiver has some choice in what they do with that comment or image. The sender (you) have much less of a choice in what happens with that comment or image. Once you send it, it is out there. Even if your account is private, it is out there. You see, anything you 'post' will sit on a cloud. Even if you delete it – it is not gone. It may disappear from your device, but it is certainly not gone. It can, and certainly would be retrieved, if that information was ever needed by the police or anyone in high places.

Without wishing to scare you or have you in a permanently heightened state of paranoia, please be mindful and cautious about what you post. But, let's take this to a lower level. Assuming you don't become the next prime minister or police commissioner - would you be happy for your employer, children, mother-in-law, students or spouse to see everything you post? Also, are you giving others the choice in whether they want their photo of the drunken night in town posted all over social media for all (including their boss) to see. I have had other people post pictures of my children on social media, without asking my permission. I would rather that didn't happen, but I don't have full control over that.

Now, consider two things; a) you may not know what your future holds or where God is taking you or how he wants to use you. How much damage could be done by a photo in your past that has long been forgotten. A little while back, I was curious about the cast of a very popular TV show that aired back in the 1990's. I did an online search and was reading and looking at images of the cast. One image (for which she had posed and was smiling at the camera) popped up that was, let's say, borderline pornography. That same cast member is now an activist and children's writer for black historical figures. I'm not sure she would want those same children that she is trying to educate to see her historical image. She took a different direction in life and seems to be doing well – my point is, we do not know what path we will take in the future and so we should be cautious about posting comments and images that could incriminate us in the future; b) when seeking a partner (or having met one) curiosity, or wisdom, may lead you to search their social media pages. What would he/she find on yours? Drunken nights out? Fondling photos with a variety of different people? Comments and slogans reflective of when you were in a bit of a dark place? Scantily clad, arms aloft, whistle-blowing images of you at that carnival when it was just too hot to wear anything more than underwear? What questions would your images or comments leave in their mind about the person they have just met?

Social media is not negative – use it positively, always considering the end goal.

4
YOU TOUCH IT, YOU BREAK IT, YOU BOUGHT IT!

You may have already guessed – this chapter focuses on sex, intimacy and self-awareness. Is it odd to cover this subject in a book about singleness? Especially a Christian book? Possibly, but we *are* going to go there! You see, there is such a broad spectrum of people who are single. There are those who have never been in a relationship and/or have never had any sexual interaction. There are those who have had plenty of sex with either one or several partners. And then, there are those in-between. As well as the personal experiences, or lack of them, there are also the external influences; movies, pornography, books and magazines etc. So, let's delve in.

Physical Requirements

Prior to meeting me, Rob had a list of physical requirements regarding the woman he would choose to marry. She needed to be, amongst other things, dark-skinned with long hair. Along came 'me'. I am light-skinned and at the time I had short hair. I didn't meet his physical requirements and yet we have been married for 13 years. What happened there? Did he settle for something (or someone) other than his personal desire? Did his physical desire become less important as he got to know me? Was he wise enough to not allow his personal preference to prevent him from exploring beyond the surface? Or was his physical desire born out of imagery that wasn't essential or relevant?

Here are some questions to get you thinking about physical preferences:

Is <u>physical</u> attraction important in choosing a life partner? Why?

_____

_____

_____

_____

_____

_____

Is it okay (as a Christian) to find your partner sexy?

_____

_____

_____

_____

_____

_____

_____

Are your physical requirements for a partner limiting your choices?

_____

_____

_____

_____

_____

_____

Physical preferences can exist for a variety of reasons. You may prefer someone tall because you are tall. You may prefer someone tall because you are short, and you would like your children to have the opportunity to be taller! You may prefer a particular race, or like Rob, a particular skin tone within a particular race. Whatever your reasons, I would like you to ask yourself, why? Often, there are reasons why we conclude that a particular 'type' is right for us.

One of the most common that we come across, Rob and I, is culture. Culture often dictates that an individual remains within their own culture to find a partner. Parental influence has a huge part to play and many will respect their parents and their culture and seek a mate accordingly.

Over the years of teaching couples who are preparing for marriage, we have seen an increase in individuals from different cultures coming together in marriage. Some come with the blessing (or agreement) of parents and the wider family. Others are unable to disclose to parents the race or culture of their chosen partner. Some have bravely told their parents that they are marrying someone of a different race and/or culture (which can sometimes include a different religious belief or faith) and they have been banished from the family or threatened. All I will add on this point is that understanding is key. We all have the capability to operate in fear when something unknown to us presents itself.

Applying stereotypes is also common.

💭 Are you someone who stereotypes others and builds a persona around your knowledge (or lack of knowledge) of a person?

Men vs Women

We can all agree that a man is a man and a woman is a woman, right? We know they are different. At least we can all agree that they are physically different. But do we agree that they are mentally different? That is, men and women do not think the same way, about the same things. You may say, 'Yes, we get it!' But, I wonder whether you really do.

This image is comical, but is there any truth in it? Research says, 'Yes!' Although the content of the image above may or may not be accurate, the truth is, woman and men do think differently.

✎ Complete the Venn Diagram below applying what *you* believe to be the characteristics of men and women:

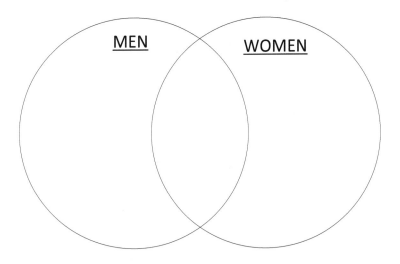

Did you find many characteristics that belonged to both men and women? Do your answers read like a list of positives for one sex and negative for the other or is there a good balance? Would you say your answers are very typical of what others would say or has your own personal experience altered your thinking?

🐾 Consider your answers and decide whether the way you think of the different sexes is healthy and balanced or whether hurt, pain and disappointment is causing you to think negatively of the opposite sex.

We know that God created man and then woman. We also know that men and women were given different tasks to fulfil. They had different roles. In today's society, the pace of life has changed, the demands of financial commitments often mean that both the man and the woman need to work away from the home. Children are spending more time away from the home also with many attending wrap-around care services or 12-hour nursery sessions. With both parents working, the home setting is naturally affected. This can mean that the expectations of a husband and wife can become blurry. If a couple decide that they will share the house chores equally, the expectation can be that both will perform their duties equally well and with the same execution.

Now, consider the above but apply it to sex and intimacy. Will you expect your husband or wife to display the same levels of affection, attention, time and detail to your intimacy as you do? Also, is there an expectation that the levels of intimacy that you would like to see displayed would already be in place when you marry, or are you prepared to grow in this area together as your marriage progresses?

One particular area that I would briefly like to mention here is the woman's monthly cycle. How a woman's hormones can be affected throughout any given month is a mystery that not even the woman can explain oftentimes. Put in the simplest terms possible, if you can imagine the month broken up into weeks:

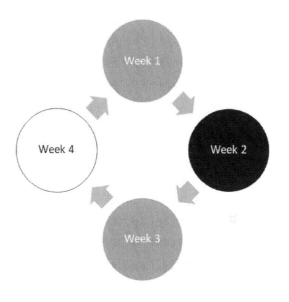

Week 1 – Proceed with extreme caution!

Week 2 – No entry!

Week 3 – Proceed with caution (having tested the waters!)

Week 4 – All clear for entry!

Now guys, this should be your worst-case scenario when no other factors are involved. Every woman is an individual and every month may offer you something alternative to this. There is also medication available (I kid you not!) My best advice to you is to get to know your wife – her needs, her reactions, her triggers, her desires and her patterns. Avoiding her until it all goes away is not advisable. Ask her questions and discuss between you the best way to deal with this area of your relationship.

Ladies, a word to you. Would it be acceptable if your man flew of the handle at the slightest thing, grunted his way through the day (several days, in fact) pushed you away and refused your advances for 3 weeks out of 4 every month and hurled abuse at you whenever you came into a room? Whilst I am fully aware that hormonal changes can cause changes in behavior and that we do not choose to behave this way, we do have self-control and communication skills that allow us to not behave like silverbacks who are threatened by predators. Feeling low, or weepy is one thing but an axe-wielding maniac is not acceptable, under any circumstances. If your husband and/or children have to hide in their rooms every month to avoid being clubbed over the head - seek medical help! Jokes aside, it really isn't okay to make someone's life miserable because you are not feeling yourself. Get help and include your husband in your thought process. He needs to be part of the solution too.

Acceptance

How accepting are you of others? Do you find it easy to accept the way others behave? Are you able to consider that other people will do things in an alternative way to you? Are you okay with that? When engaging with single people who are seeking partners, we often hear people say things like, 'From the minute I saw him, I noticed he did this thing with his neck. It just put me off straight away. I won't be seeing him again!' Now, of course, it is entirely your decision whether or not to meet someone for a second date, but is it possible that when two people meet for the first time, there may be some unusual behavior? Could nerves be part of the equation? Also, consider that some people will habitually do what they have always done because there has been no reason to alter that behavior.

When I met Rob, he had a pattern of behavior that had me considering whether my future with him would have me following the same pattern.

Every Sunday, following the church service, Rob would immediately visit two or three of his family members in succession and then arrive at his home late at night, in time for bed. He told me he did this every week and I was concerned that he would expect me to do the same once we were married. It transpired that Rob would go to the first family member for lunch straight after the service, stay a while, then leave to visit the next family member where he would have dinner. The third would give him a container of food for the next day and off he would go, fed, loved-up and ready for the week ahead. A huge part of that process was Rob receiving the love and attention of his family, not just being fed by them. In my mind, I wanted our Sunday afternoons to be evenly distributed between family, relaxation, activities, visiting friends etc. but what I saw in Rob was a habitual practice which had existed long before I came on the scene, being lived out via circumstance. Once we started to see other regularly, Rob's pattern changed, and we spent more time together, much of which was spent planning for our future.

My intolerance during the initial stages of our relationship almost caused me to draw conclusions based on what was a circumstantial practice. Had I not stuck around to discover that Rob's practice was indeed circumstantial, I certainly would have missed out on my greatest, God-given blessing to date.

How tolerant are you? *(Circle your answer)*

(Not at all) 1   2   3   4   5   6   7   8   9   10 *(Extremely)*

How can you become more accepting of others?

_____

_____

_____

_____

_____

_____

✏️ What could you change about yourself that would make you more accepting to others?

_____

_____

_____

_____

_____

_____

_____

Bear in mind, when considering behaviors that may frustrate you about the opposite sex, it could be the very thing that is needed in your relationship, i.e. 'He's just too laid back!' – His calming nature may be what is needed to calm you down. 'She talks a lot!'– You don't communicate enough!

The opposite can also be true. The very thing you love about your partner, can also be the thing that frustrates you at times. Rob often shares that he loves the fact that I am opinionated and that I have a view about pretty much everything but, at times, it drives him nuts. There are times when he just needs me to listen. For example, when he comes home and sits opposite me in the kitchen and just wants to share about his day. All he needs me to do is listen, but, no. I rant on and on about what should be done to fix an issue, or I build concepts around an idea that he has shared and start pulling out my laptop to devise a business plan. At those times, he just needs me to focus on his need (which is to listen). I'm still learning!

Sex

What does sex mean to you? Does this seem like an odd question? Probably, but sex means different things to different people. We could all probably describe the sexual act, as in what happens during sex, but I guarantee we all have a different image in our minds when we think about sex. Some will think of media images they have seen, i.e. movies, pornography etc. Some may think of their own past experiences. Some may have very negative experiences attached to sex, i.e. abuse or rape. Some will have very romanticized images in their mind developed from romantic novels for example, whilst others, may visualize animalistic behavior in connection with sex. The mental images differ for each individual.

In the bible, sex is referred to in a variety of ways. Many of the references involve prostitutes or homosexuality. Sex, in these cases are referred to in the form of teaching or prevention. Song of songs, however, displays sex in the form of tender love-making with beauty and delight being the focal emphasis. God created sex to be pleasurable for a man and his wife. The world has distorted sex, which, by the way, became distorted in the biblical era, not in more recent decades as some would have us believe. God could have created sex purely for reproduction, but He formed and created us in such a way that we could derive pleasure from *'being'* with our husband or wife.

Sex, and the sexual act, are different for a man and a woman, we are formed differently, and our different parts serve a different purpose. Internally, we are different too. Our emotions and expressions differ in relation to sex. The way a woman feels and expresses herself will be different to her husband, and vice versa. I encourage you be open and have dialogue with your partner at varying levels as you progress through your relationship so that sex is not a taboo subject for you in your marriage. Now, please exercise caution and wisdom when you decide to have these talks. First and second dates are not the time to go there! And, the content of your discussion must be appropriate and relevant.

As Rob and I prepared for our wedding we would ask each other how we felt about the fact that we would soon be having sex. We asked each other if we felt nervous about our impending wedding night, and so on. We did not, (and never have), ask each other about our sexual history. Once we were married we would talk about what we liked and what we weren't so keen on. We would give feedback to each other and encourage each other, ensuring that we were meeting each other's needs. This became an integral part of our intimacy.

In my singleness, sex wasn't really a battle for me. I found that if I watched movies with sexual scenes in them, it would awaken something in me – so I avoided watching those scenes. I am no saint! I just know myself. If I like something, I tend to consume myself with it. I will go headlong, all in! So, I kept sexual content off the agenda. However, I had friends, one in particular, who was burning with an intense desire for sex. She was single, and she was struggling. So much so, that she was prepared to risk everything, even another man's marriage to have one night of passion to fulfil her desire. This opened my eyes to the 'pull' and enticement that sex has over some people. It is very real.

Now to the unmarried and the widows I say: It is good for them to stay unmarried, as I do. But if they cannot control themselves, they should marry, for it is better to marry than to burn with passion.

1 Cor 7:8-10 (NIV)

Know yourself! If movies and images are causing you to think and dream about sex, make steps to prevent these things from being in your life until you are in a position to act on them.

7 STEPS TO RESISTING SEXUAL TEMPTATION

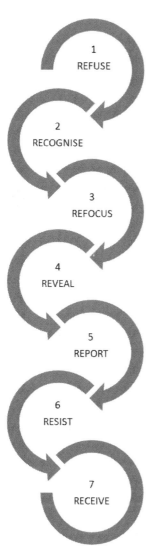

1 If you believe what the bible says, and you desire to remain a virgin until you marry, do not compromise and do what others are doing.

2 If you are engaging in sexual activity, admit to yourself that this is not the plan you had for yourself.

3 We serve a forgiving God. Ask for forgiveness and refocus. But do not continue to repeat your sin. God is not to be played with!

4 Do not continue in silence. What is kept in the dark will fester and grow.

5 Seek a mentor and invite them to come alongside you as you work through your temptation

6 Keep your eyes and your mind from being fed with the images that will tempt you. Put boundaries in place.

7 Knowing you have conducted yourself appropriately will make your reward sweeter. No guilt. No shame!

Dear friend, pay close attention to this, my wisdom;
listen very closely to the way I see it.
Then you'll acquire a taste for good sense; what I tell
you will keep you out of trouble.

The lips of a seductive woman are oh so sweet, her
soft words are oh so smooth.
But it won't be long before she's gravel in your
mouth, a pain in your gut, a wound in your heart.
She's dancing down the primrose path to Death; she's
headed straight for Hell and taking you with her. She
hasn't a clue about Real Life, about who she is or
where she's going.

So, my friend, listen closely; don't treat my words
casually. Keep your distance from such a woman;
Absolutely stay out of her neighbourhood.

You don't want to squander your wonderful life, to
waste your precious life among the hard-hearted.
Why should you allow strangers to take advantage of
you?

Why be exploited by those who care nothing for you?
You don't want to end your life full of regrets, nothing
but sin and bones,
Saying, "Oh, why didn't I do what they told me? Why
did I reject a disciplined life?
Why didn't I listen to my mentors, or take my
teachers seriously?
My life is ruined!
I haven't one blessed thing to show for my life!"

Do you know the saying, "Drink from your own rain barrel, draw water from your own spring-fed well"? It's true. Otherwise, you may one day come home and find your barrel empty and your well polluted.

Your spring water is for you and you only, not to be passed around among strangers.
Bless your fresh-flowing fountain! Enjoy the wife you married as a young man!
Lovely as an angel, beautiful as a rose—don't ever quit taking delight in her body.
Never take her love for granted!

Why would you trade enduring intimacies for cheap thrills with a whore?
For dalliance with a promiscuous stranger?

Mark well that GOD doesn't miss a move you make; he's aware of every step you take.
The shadow of your sin will overtake you; you'll find yourself stumbling all over yourself in the dark.
Death is the reward of an undisciplined life; your foolish decisions trap you in a dead end.

Proverbs 5 (MSG)

Do you not know that your bodies are members of Christ himself? Shall I then take the members of Christ and unite them with a prostitute? Never! Do you not know that he who unites himself with a prostitute is one with her in body? For it is said, "The two will *become one flesh." But whoever is united with the Lord is one with him in spirit.*

Flee from sexual immorality. All other sins a person commits are outside the body, but whoever sins sexually, sins against their own body. Do you not know that your bodies are temples of the Holy Spirit, who is in you, whom you have received from God? You are not your own; you were bought at a price. Therefore, honour God with your bodies.

1 Cor 6:15-20 (NIV)

As mentioned previously, sex was created and designed by God as a pleasurable act between a husband and his wife. In many cases, including within marriage, sex is being used as a form of power. There are cases where those who have had little or no control over their circumstances begin to use sex as a form of power.

One young man, whilst Rob and I sat with him and talked about his childhood, revealed that he had not had any control over what happened to him when he was young. People had come and gone in his life and he had had to go along with whatever circumstance he found himself in. As he grew older and became of age, he discovered that he could control women by enticing them and drawing them in, to the point of desiring him. He would then sexually arouse them to the point where they would be prepared to do anything, and he would then feel a sense of control and power.

As he spoke with us, he appeared ashamed of his behavior. He had no desire to hurt these women. In fact, his desire to have some control over his life was becoming entwined with the desire to be wanted and needed. He longed for a committed relationship where he could be accepted, loved, desired, purposeful and giving. But he was struggling to separate the need for power and the need for love.

Often, a woman will use sex as a tool for control, denying her husband sex if he has not ticked all the right boxes that day, or enticing him with sex as a reward.

Ladies, our husbands are not pets that receive a 'treat' as a reward for good behavior. Sex is not your right to withhold or distribute as you see fit.

Sex within marriage is a requirement, not a reward. A married man *needs* sex to function as he should. Look at what the bible says about withholding sex:

> Sexual drives are strong, but marriage is strong enough to contain them and provide for a balanced and fulfilling sexual life in a world of sexual disorder. The marriage bed must be a place of mutuality—the husband seeking to satisfy his wife, the wife seeking to satisfy her husband. Marriage is not a place to "stand up for your rights." Marriage is a decision to serve the other, whether in bed or out. Abstaining from sex is permissible for a period of time if you both agree to it, and if it's for the purposes of prayer and fasting—but only for such times. Then come back together again.
>
> **1 Cor 7:2-6 (MSG)**

Does this mean a man has the right to demand sex as and when he wants it? Of course not. But the times of withholding tend to increase when all is not well within your marriage. The better the marriage, the better your intimacy will be with your spouse.

Intimacy

Sex and intimacy are not the same. Does that come as a surprise to you?

Sex is an act that is carried out between two people. Those two people may not be in love with each other. They may not even know each other. Sex can also take place when there is no consent.

Intimacy, on the other hand, is an affection for another person that permeates through their entire relationship and touches *every* aspect of their lives. In a good, healthy, God-centered relationship, intimacy will be present in every aspect of your interaction.

Let's look at a few 'categories' of the marriage relationship and emphasize the presence of intimacy:

Communication:

Speaking with each other, whether face to face, via messaging or in written form, your words should be spoken with love, tenderness, thoughtfulness and encouragement. Edification should be your goal when speaking with your spouse – not tearing down or belittling. Request, rather than command. Consider their thoughts and feelings in your decision making, trying to make your plans work for all involved.

Prayer:

Whether you are praying with your spouse, alone or with others, your prayers should be heartfelt, encouraging words that encourage your partner to be all that God has called them to be. Prayer time is not the time to ask God to 'fix' all that you deem to be wrong with your spouse. It is also not the time to highlight the current unresolved issue you may be trying to work through, hoping that he'll get the message as you prayer aloud with him, i.e. 'Lord, help Simon to understand that you have given him the ability to communicate and that he should use that ability to try and reflect your son Jesus so that we may put aside that which is not of you and focus on being upright and Godly...'

Children:

As you raise your children, agree to do this in partnership. Agree, where possible, how you will reward them and how you will discipline them. Do not encourage them to favor one of you over the other but understand that your relationship with them will be different. Make every effort to spend family time together eating, doing activities, doing the bed time routine etc. Allow your children to see and hear you making plans together. Allow them to witness you laughing together, hugging each other and making plans for their future. Include them in these things.

Sex:

Intimacy is never 'off the table' so sex should be the culmination of your intimacy. As you arise in the morning, greet each other and begin to serve one another with a cup of tea in bed, ironing a shirt or a skirt, sharing that slice of toast (whatever works for you). Message each other throughout the day if you are unable to speak. Send encouraging messages of love and appreciation to each other, not just factual messages – 'Can you pick up some milk on your way home' or 'Train is late!'. Make time to listen to each other when you arrive home. Cook together. Share a bath. Snuggle together and watch a movie. Sex, after all that, should be mind-blowing!

Finance:

Be open about your finances. Make plans for holidays or new cars etc. together. Encourage and reward each other when you have achieved a financial goal, i.e. paying off that credit card which took some sacrifices. Make long-term plans about what you would both like to see your money spent on. If one of you is better at money management than the other, encourage and appreciate that person for keeping your finances in order.

Conflict:

It may not be easy to be intimate when there is conflict, but it is possible. Even when you are angry you can respect and value your spouse. Anger does not mean that love is removed (even though it can feel that way). When you have conflict, do not shout, swear, insult or threaten your spouse. Do not try to 'win' by putting them down or raking up past hurts. Speak the truth but speak it in love. Make every effort to put aside that which your head wants to say. Speak that which is helpful for resolution. Do not go over and over the facts of the argument – state the facts and move on to the resolution. Decide how you both want to move forward and try not to remain in a silent state for very long. Resume normal activity and continue to engage with each other so that what is ahead is magnified and what is behind is minimized.

This intimacy does not switch on when you say, 'I will'. It develops throughout your courtship and continues to develop throughout your marriage. In your singleness, you should begin to develop yourself so that you are prepared for the dual role of partnership.

I'm not going to tell you that intimacy will be simple during courtship. It won't be, for many of you. What I will tell you is, you will need to be responsible, you will need to apply wisdom and you will be answerable to God for what (or who) he has placed in your care.

Let's focus on wisdom for a moment.

Many younger couples, at the early stage of their relationship, ask us about our views on kissing before marriage. We simply tell them – if kissing stops at kissing, then kiss! Kissing triggers different levels of stimulation for different people.

Some can kiss and feel loved. Some kiss and feel tingly. Some kiss and feel aroused. Some kiss and feel nothing. Where are you when it comes to kissing? And, where is your partner? Possibly, not in the same place. Also, when you are kissing, where are your hands? By your sides? On her waist? Wrapped around her back? On her breast? Above her clothes or below her clothes? You see my point, right? Kissing tends to not only involve lips.

What about this question? Can we stay at each other's houses overnight? My question would be, 'Why?' What's wrong with your house? There are a number of reasons given as to why a dating couple would decide to stay overnight – even in separate rooms. None of them really justify the absolute need in my book. 'We have a long-distance relationship and we tend to spend one weekend a month together.' Okay. I understand. But factor in the cost of a hotel and relieve yourself of the pressure or temptation to be in each other's bedroom space. This may seem harsh, I know. But, when temptation gets the better of you or the relationship doesn't work out – or both, you are now left with a feeling of regret. Plan well and wait for the appointed time.

Holidaying together is another question we often have put to us. In short, I would say, holidaying with friends in groups is an option. Romantic holidays with just the two of you present is a hot bed of temptation. Especially if there is sun, sea and swimsuits in the mix. Flee temptation! Do not swing the doors wide open and invite temptation and his friends to come and party on your patio! Wait!

Set boundaries and do your utmost to stick to them. Ensure that your use of language is appropriate so that your partner is not made to feel as though they are burning every time they are with you. You may feel that it is flattering that your partner desires you so much that they are struggling to be around you but, believe me, it is not fun for them – and that struggle could cause them to sin. You wouldn't want that for them. Would you?

The way you dress can also be a form of temptation for your partner. Exposed cleavage and super tight clothing don't leave much to the imagination.

If you are a tactile person, be mindful that your touch may be enough to send tingles up and down your partners spine.

Just as with marriage, your dating and courting should be approached from a mind-set that offers help to your partner – not hindrance. You are there to uphold your partner and help them to succeed and thrive, not to tear them down and cause them to fail.

God's order for dating & marriage

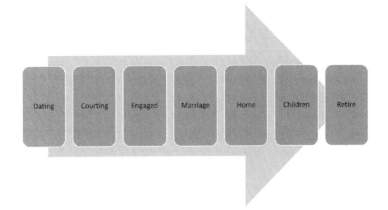

Dating   Courting   Engaged   Marriage   Home   Children   Retire

In God's perfect plan, this would be the order and process for our romantic relationships:

Beginning with singleness, we would *date* and decide who we want to choose as our life long partner. *Courting* would follow as you move forward in your commitment to build a life together. *Engagement* is the promise to *marry* after which you move in together and build your *home* as a married couple. *Children* (should you choose to have them or are blessed with them) are then added and you go about the business of raising them. *Retirement* comes as the final stage of life here on earth.

I have made these stages seem very simple and straightforward. Idealistic, some would say. But you get the idea. I realize that our lives do not always follow this perfect, progressive pattern. I am also aware that we sometimes do not have control over every aspect of our lives. But, the point I am trying to emphasize is, the original plan for our lives was this order, although, in biblical times, the first five stages took place all in one day, with no bridal shower, stag do, church, priest or white dress. Nevertheless, they were still completed in order. *Read Genesis 24.*

We may not have complete control over the stages of our lives, i.e. some may not marry. Some may not have children. But, we do have control over the order in which we complete the stages. We do have a choice in whether we choose to live with someone outside of marriage. We do have a choice in whether we have consensual sex with someone outside of marriage. You may say, 'I have no control whether he proposes to me!' Whilst that may be true, you do have a choice in whether you progress to the later stages without being engaged.

There was a time when you could not join your local gym and complete a work-out until you had completed an intensive induction. If you wanted to work-out, you had no option but to complete the induction. So, you completed the induction and you were then permitted to use the gym. In many establishments, that has now changed. You are now warned of the dangers of using the gym equipment without having been shown how to do so, but the onus is on you to keep yourself safe. They are plenty of warnings displayed about the dangers of using the equipment without training and those warning are usually followed by disclaimers.

The same appears to be happening in relation to dating, sex, co-habitation, children outside of wedlock etc. We are warned about the 'dangers' involved but the onus is on the individual to recognize the risks.

Attention!

A healthy, loving relationship requires both partners to be attentive to each other's needs.

'I've told you that 'I Love You'. If that ever changes I'll let you know!'

Is this acceptable? Of course not. Both you and your partner deserve far more than this reactive, non-attentive approach. Even a plant will die away if it is not attended to. How much more, you and I? We all need food, water and fresh air, but we need so much more than that to exist in a life-long, committed relationship. Anything that requires growth needs a level of attention. Some require higher levels than others, but we all need a good measure to not just to exist, or even grow. We need to thrive!

Remember, the life is in the roots! We can't see the damage that is being caused until the plant or tree begins to show signs of damage or neglect. Keep the 'roots' healthy and the plant/tree wife/husband will thrive.

How?

Check on them. Regularly. Be assertive. Keep your eyes open for signs of decay. Has his/her appearance changed? Keep listening to the use of language or tone. When you hold each other, is the response lesser or looser than it used to be? Are you communicating well – even when you are absent from each other. If you know your partner well, you will know when changes occur.

🍂 Remember – a healthy, shiny, upstanding, blossoming plant is far more attractive than a droopy, crispy, sagging, dying plant. Which would you rather be married to?

Love language

Do you know your love language?

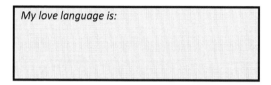

My love language is:

If the answer is no, discover what it is before you start dating! If your love language is *receiving gifts* it would be better to discover whether your date is stingy and miserly or generous and giving before you commit to a lifelong relationship.

We often make the mistake of offering love to others in the same format that we want to receive it. We all desire love to be displayed in different ways and if you know what your love language is you can communicate your preferences to your partner.

Please don't fall into the trap of thinking that your partner should just *know* how you want to be loved. You are setting them up to fail. Teach each other how you want to be loved, otherwise you could actually push your partner away rather than drawing closer together.

Example: a beautiful woman was married to a man that liked to bring his wife flowers regularly. Sometimes, he would also buy her shoes or chocolates, even jewelry on occasion. Nothing wrong with that, right? What he didn't realize was, his wife had been abandoned by her father when she was a teenager. When her father later contacted her from overseas, he would send her gifts to try and make up for his absence. She didn't want his presents – she wanted his presence. Now, she is married to a kind-hearted man who just wants his wife to know that he loves her and is thinking of her when they are apart from each other. Unfortunately, his gifts remind her of her estranged father and makes her feel sad and angry.

Is it the husband's fault that his wife feels that way about his gifts? Absolutely not! But she has not told him how it makes her feel because she doesn't want to make him feel bad, because, above all, he is doing something beautiful for her. She also feels that she has left it too long now to tell him how his gifts make her feel. She doesn't want to embarrass him. So, here we have two wonderful people, trying to love each other, but not knowing how to display it. Such a shame.

Will you enter into and exist in a relationship where your partner doesn't know how to love you?

To discover your love language, check out: www.5lovelanguages.com or purchase a copy of Gary Chapman's book *The 5 Love Languages*.

5
SPRINT OR MARATHON?

Despite my reliance on God to prepare me for my husband and my assurance that He would deliver him, I seemed to bypass the *'all in God's timing'* reassurances and developed in my head a time-frame for how my journey from dating to marriage would all work out. Did I mention that I like to plan?

As mentioned earlier, I had my five-year plan.

Rob's plan was slightly different. Having been in relationships that had not led to finding the person he wanted to spend the rest of his life with, in frustration, Rob had declared to God, aloud, 'Right God, you know what? I am done with women! From now on, it's just me and you!' Two weeks later, we began speaking. Two weeks after that, he knew I was 'the one'. Eleven months later we were married.

So much for the plan! Question is, who sets the pace? You or God?

It's always good to have a plan, but how flexible are you? Would you miss out on your blessing if you preferred a long courtship and God said, now! Would you potentially chase off a potential spouse by moving too quickly?

The Long and the Short of it!

✎ Think about, and list below, the reasons why you may prefer a long courtship or a short courtship. Be honest! As much as I didn't want to rush into anything, I knew that, with every month that passed, I had one less egg with which to produce children. And yet, I felt more comfortable with a long courtship as I felt I would know my future husband better if we dated for a longer period.

Long	**Short**

Now, ask yourself, 'Am I prepared to be flexible or am I immoveable in this area of my life?'

The One!

The age-old question when talking about relationships is, 'Do you believe there is the one?' Some believe they are destined to meet the one person that has been assigned for them from the beginning of time. Others believe they can choose whomever they like. The bible doesn't say that there is one woman assigned to each man.

Abraham, in Genesis 24, asked his servant to go and find a wife for his son Isaac. He gave him clear instructions on the type of woman he wanted for his son, but he did not say, 'Go and get Rebekah whom has been assigned to marry my son.'

The bible also states,

> *'A wife is bound to her husband as long as he lives. If her husband dies, she is free to marry anyone she wishes, but only if he loves the Lord.'*

> **I Cor 7:39 (NLT)**

Much like every other decision, including salvation, we are free to choose whom we wish to marry, but the bible guides us in making the choice – not so much with the *actual* individual but the *type* of individual.

> Don't become partners with those who reject God. How can you make a partnership out of right and wrong? That's not partnership; that's war. Is light best friends with dark? Does Christ go strolling with the Devil? Do trust and mistrust hold hands? Who would think of setting up pagan idols in God's holy Temple? But that is exactly what we are, each of us a temple in whom God lives.
>
> **2 Cor 6:14-18 (MSG)**

Just as Abraham instructed his servant regarding a wife for his son, imagine you were doing the same. Use the radial below to create a list of criteria that you would give to a friend to find you a husband or wife:

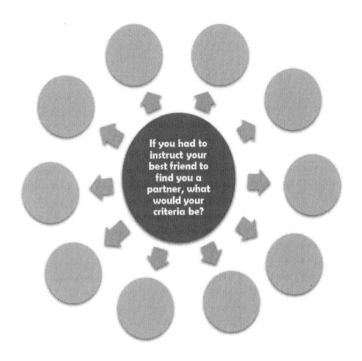

If you had to instruct your best friend to find you a partner, what would your criteria be?

Whose voice?

Often, our choice of partner is influenced by those around us or by images and impressions via the media. Stereotypes and cultural norms are fed to us as we grow and mature and we absorb them, often without realizing.

Is your choice of life partner entirely your

decision? Who (or what) is influencing your decision?

With (1) representing no influence whatsoever and (10) representing total control, complete the chart below bearing the following in mind:

Parents – Parents can have an enormous influence on the person we choose. They may allow you to choose the person and then inform you whether they approve of your choice. Some parents may want to choose for you. Some may strongly disapprove of your choice based on race, culture, age, education, religion, character, to name just a few.

Partner – If you are already in a relationship, your partner may be trying to influence whether you marry them. You may be unsure. You are running a marathon whilst he/she is sprinting!

Friends – Friends may approve or disapprove of your partner for a variety of reasons. They may also try to influence the type of person you date based on their needs. Be cautious but open when it comes to the opinion of friends. Some may not want to release you into your marriage because of how it will change your relationship with them. Some may want you to marry someone because they are fun, and they fit into their circle perfectly – but is that person right for you and for where you are going in life?

Media – The media can be one of the biggest influences when it comes to relationships. Romantic movies paint the perfect picture with the happy ending. Pornography displays sex as an insatiable act that can be fulfilled if you are married (sex on tap). Posters and magazines portray images of sexy couples, always looking perfect and passionate – even when they are at the supermarket or in the garden. Music videos, computer games, apps, the internet, even radio will make people seem super-sexy and joyful at all times. When we don't experience these things in our relationships, we can quickly become dejected.

God – The bible contains a lot of teaching

about marriage, including instructions for husbands and wives. Some will see it as outdated, often due to the pace of society and constant changes in belief systems etc. Ecclesiastes tells us 'there is nothing new under the sun', and this is true. Much of what we see happening in society today also took place in biblical times. The difference is, today's society has become more accepting of certain behaviors and/or practices, so they have become more visible – but they are not new.

Whose voice?

10				
9				
8				
7				
6				
5				
4				
3				
2				
1				
0				
Parents	Partner	Friends	Media	God

Are you surprised by any of your answers? Were you totally honest with yourself? Whether you like what you see, once you complete the chart, or not, the fact is external influences do feature in our decision making regarding our life partner. The question is, are they the right influences?

Accountability

What does accountability mean to you? Some think of counselling sessions with a clipboard, a white coat and an interrogation into their personal life. Some imagine a short, timed session where you confess your 'sins' and plead for forgiveness.

Accountability should be a relationship with someone who is more advanced in life than you are who can listen, guide, correct and nurture you to become the better version of you. The person you are accountable to should be someone who's lifestyle, output and influence is positive, appropriate and God-fearing.

If you are in a relationship, it is a good idea to seek a couple to be accountable to. Being able to receive the views, opinions and guidance of both the male and female will enhance your relationship.

Rob and I have rules when we mentor couples or individuals. Firstly, we mentor couples together. Rob mentors' individual (or groups of males) and I mentor individual (or groups of) females. It is not a good idea for me to mentor a guy and try to guide him as he shares his struggles with masturbation. Wisdom must be applied. If a male requires a female perspective Rob and I will meet him together.

Secondly, we do make it clear that we will not be used as sounding boards. We have encountered couples that just want to air their grievances in front of an audience so that we can then 'vote' and decide who is in the wrong.

Thirdly, we must see change. Even if it is slow, gradual change. But, we will not spend valuable time with a couple, advising and guiding them, praying with them, etc. just for them to return on their next visit and repeat the same behaviors. There must be a willingness to grow or we are all wasting time!

Fourthly, respect must be shown to all parties involved. We will not disrespect an individual or couple by insulting them or belittling them etc. We expect to also be respected by not being shouted at or spoken to aggressively. We also request that couples do not shout or disrespect each other whilst in our presence. Ideally couples wouldn't shout at each other and disrespect each other period! We also ask that our time would be respected – turning up late for an appointment is disrespectful – whichever way you look at it.

Finally, and naturally, confidentiality is key. If we are to share our personal experiences with someone and they are to open up to us about their personal lives, we must hold all that is said in total confidence.

Accountability is ideally formed through relationship. Unlike counselling, a relationship of mentor and mentee should develop or already be in place in order to guide an individual or couple through a stage, or stages, of life.

How do you find someone to be accountable to? Firstly, pray for God to reveal someone to you that can be a part of your development. Small groups are a good place to discover whether there might be someone to guide you as you may already interact with someone there. If you serve on a particular ministry or team within your church, is there someone there that might develop into a mentor?

Time is important when mentoring someone. A person who is extremely busy with very little free time in their diary may struggle to make the time to mentor someone.

Approaching a perfect stranger and asking them to mentor you is not advisable. You may admire them from afar but if there is no relationship it may be best to wait and watch. Always remain prayerful, God will reveal someone to you as he knows your needs long before you do.

Why be accountable?

These quotes help to explain the purpose of accountability:

You will only hold yourself accountable for goals that others know about. Tell someone what you are up to.

Accountability is the glue that ties commitment to results.

*It is not only what we do, but also what we do not do, for which we are accountable.
(Moliere)*

*Accountability breeds response-ability.
(Steven Covey)*

In all his scheming, the wicked person arrogantly thinks, "There is no accountability, since there's no God."

Psalms 10:4 (CSB)

✎ What are your views on counselling?

_____

_____

_____

_____

_____

_____

✎ What are your views on accountability?

_____

_____

_____

_____

_____

_____

Are you accountable to or mentored by anyone? Is it beneficial?

_____

_____

_____

_____

_____

_____

Remember: Counselling and accountability should not be a form of interrogation. Whilst counselling may feel more formal with pre-set sessions and more probing etc. you should not feel like you are in a court of law. It should feel beneficial and useful and should stimulate growth.

Accountability or mentoring should develop via relationship and should have more of an ease surrounding the relationship. Think of coffee & cake or a meal with a respected 'friend' who is, maybe, older than you but certainly ahead of where you are in terms of the area that you wish to focus on, i.e. relationships, finance management, parenting, etc.

6
MAKE UP OR BREAK UP?

"I mean, he's not perfect. No-one is though, right? What if I break up with him just to find that there isn't anyone better out there. Better the devil you know, ay?"

Sound familiar?

Do you want to be married or in a relationship with the devil?

Sometimes, people feel that staying in the same relationship, even if it makes them unhappy, is better than starting again or, worse still, never meeting anyone else. Fear is a major factor here. If you truly believe that God has the best for you, why would you settle for less?

Why do we stay in relationships that are not right for us?

Write down reasons why you might feel obliged or pressured to stay in a relationship that does not feel right to you.

Here are just a few of the reasons (or excuses) we have heard during our time of mentoring couples:

- I have invested too much time in this relationship to just walk away now.
- My parents feel she is the right one for me.
- I think he may fall away from church if I am not there to encourage him.
- His children have got used to having me around.
- We truly believe God has called us to be together.
- We have the same vision for mission.
- He just does it for me.
- For all that she does that drives me absolutely crazy, I've got used to having her around.
- She's fit.

If you hear yourself saying similar things regarding relationships, consider being with that person for the rest of your life.

The late Dr Miles Munroe said, 'Nothing magic happens at the altar. If your spouse is lazy when they walk up the aisle, they'll still be lazy when they walk back down it with you.' I'm paraphrasing, but what Dr Myles said really stuck with me. We often hope for change, but what if that change never comes. That quality we see in our partner that really grates on our last nerve – imagine that for the rest of your life together. When I quote Dr Myles, I now extend his phrase with my own – 'There is no magic but there is a magnifying glass and that magnifying glass will highlight all their irritating habits by a thousand.' These habits may change over time – but they may not.

Now, this doesn't mean that you go searching for someone who is perfect. He/she does not exist. Neither are you perfect. You will also have irritating habits that will take your partner to the edge and back sometimes. We all have them. My point is, that inner feeling that is telling you that this is not right for you – listen to it. If you remove God from the equation when choosing your life partner, you are on your own, and what may seem attractive and appealing to you now may not be what you need in 10 or 20 years' time.

Submit yourselves, then, to God. Resist the devil, and he will flee from you.

James 4:7 (NIV)

Love never gives up.
Love cares more for others than for self.
Love doesn't want what it doesn't have.
Love doesn't strut,
Doesn't have a swelled head,
Doesn't force itself on others,
Isn't always "me first,"
Doesn't fly off the handle,
Doesn't keep score of the sins of others,
Doesn't revel when others grovel,
Takes pleasure in the flowering of truth,
Puts up with anything,
Trusts God always,
Always looks for the best,
Never looks back,
But keeps going to the end.

1 Cor 13:4-7 (MSG)

Fix or flee?

I'd like to just touch on some behaviors that can display themselves in relationships;

- Aggression
- Possessiveness
- Isolation
- Control
- Coercion
- Threatening behaviour
- Violent behaviour
- Sexual violence

I will not dwell on these forms of domestic abuse as I am no expert, but what I will say is, in many cases where Rob and I have been called upon to assist in marriages where one or more of these behaviors where present, when questioned the victim has confessed that the signs of the particular behavior were present during dating. They went on to explain that they had sensed that something was not right, but they entered into marriage hoping it was nothing to worry about.

Take a look at this case study:

Zane is dating Ava. Zane is 18. He has left school but has yet to find work. He spends his days hanging with his boys but sometimes he will go to work with his uncle who has a construction business.

As Zane gets benefits and some money from his uncle, he does have money coming. in, so he always dresses well and takes care of his appearance. Zane is very attractive and tall compared to his friends, so he tends to get a lot of attention from girls and even older women.

Ava is a 16-year-old shy, quiet girl. She is very pretty, and guys often show her attention. She doesn't really enjoy the attention and tends to ignore it. After school, Ava works a few hours at the local coffee shop. Zane and his friends often hang out at the coffee shop and that is where he first saw Ava.

He kept coming into the shop to talk to her and was very charming and polite. Sometimes he would walk her home after her shift. Eventually

Ava started to look forward to Zane meeting her after work.

Once, when Zane came to the shop, a guy was trying to talk to Ava, and even though she was ignoring him as best she could, Zane got mad and blamed her for talking to the guy. That day, Zane walked Ava home and as they turned into her front garden out of view of other pedestrians, Zane pushed Ava up against the wall and with his hand around her neck warned her not to flirt with other guys and make him look stupid. Ava began to cry with fear. Zane let go of her neck and, stroking her cheek, apologized, saying, "Babe, why did you make me do that? You know I can't deal with the thought of other guys being anywhere near you. Stay away from them and I promise this will never happen again."

This is an all too familiar story. Many of you will say, 'Get out Ava!' The signs of control and aggressive behavior are there for all to see. But, what if Zane didn't put his hand around Ava's neck? What if, in a lovely, kind voice, he said to her, 'Babe, you know I can't deal with the thought of other guys being anywhere near you. I love you so much, I just want to protect you.' Is that better? Or is that a subtle form of control and possessiveness?

This, more subtle approach can leave a person feeling protected, wanted, desired etc. Before long they are wrapped up in the relationship and it becomes more and more difficult to get out.

The dangers of entering into relationships in a broken state can often lead to inappropriate behavior taking place as the victim doesn't feel strong (or whole) enough to get out. When you know who you are, and you know your self-worth you are less likely to get entangled with those who will devalue you.

Again, accountability will assist in these situations as you will have someone to talk to about how your relationship is progressing.

What am I like when I'm angry?

We all feel angry at one time or another, but we all display our anger in differing ways. Do you withdraw when you are angry and internalize your feelings? Do you become tearful? Do you write your feelings down and then close the journal? Or, do you rage and shout and throw things? Maybe you fit somewhere between?

Take a moment to self-analyze your behavior when you are angry. How would you appear to others?

Use single words to describe what you are like when you're angry?

In anger, we attempt to justify our behavior. It's as though we feel justified in behaving that way because we are angry. But, I'd like you to imagine what it must be like to live on the receiving end of your anger.

Those who tend to withdraw and remain silent in their anger often feel they are in the best 'category' when it comes to conflict resolution. They feel that they are behaving in a peaceful, non-threatening way and therefore keeping the peace. Actually, that silence and lack of responsiveness can cause your partner or those around you to become very frustrated. If they are wanting to talk things through and you are shutting down, they will become angrier because nothing is being dealt with and no progress is being made.

Whether you are in the *'we never argue'* camp or the *'we are always arguing'* camp, or somewhere in between, remember this quote:

If you ALWAYS do
what you've ALWAYS done,
you'll ALWAYS get
what you've ALWAYS got!

Many people have laid claim to this quote including Henry Ford and Albert Einstein – They all have something in common – they were/are world changers!

In conflict, if you continue to remain silent, or you continue to shout and scream without changing the outcome – you will continue to argue over the same points for years to come.

In my first book, I went into great detail about an argument that Rob and I had soon after we were married. It was an awful experience (although many who read the book thought it was hilarious) and we continued to relive it on a regular basis until we concluded that, a) this is pointless and exhausting, b) we are not enjoying one iota of this, and c) if we keep doing what we've always done, we'll keep getting what we've always got. That was the wake-up call for us. We changed the formula and got a different outcome.

Conflict is not negative if handled well. There are times when these thoughts may come to your mind in the midst of conflict;

- 'I want to resolve this, but I don't know how'

- 'I don't know what he/she is thinking'

- 'I want to reach out to him/her but what if I get rejected?'

Like this image, conflict can be exhausting if it is not progressive. There comes a point when you become tired of all the arguing or not speaking to each other and you just want to be civilized again – but you don't know how. The recovery process can begin with you. Often, we wait to see whether our partner will reach out first – and when they don't, we don't either. The silence continues and then it becomes a waiting game to see who will speak first. But the game isn't fun. It's tiring and torturous. Be the one that breaks the silence. Be the one that says, 'sorry'. Be the one that says, 'shall we talk about this?' Be the one that says 'come to bed' when your partner is laying on the sofa. Be the one to send a message during the day when you left each other angry in the morning. Your partner should learn from you that it's ok to reach out when there is conflict. If you both learn, over time, to reach out to each other during/following conflict, your relationship will be far more rewarding and harmonious.

Red Rag

In a relationship, you will very quickly learn what your partner's red rag is. There may even be a few. A red rag is a word, gesture, sound or action that causes your partner to proceed from 1 – 10 on the anger spectrum at record speed.

✎ **What is YOUR Red Rag?**

_____

_____

_____

_____

_____

_____

_____

If you recognize what your own red reg is, and you understand how it feels when someone uses it (intentionally or otherwise) to make you angry, you _should_ be less likely to use your partners red rag, just to get a reaction - you may not like the reaction you get!

SUMMARY

In my singleness, I learnt many things, many of which I can appreciate only now that I am married. Hindsight is indeed a wonderful thing!

In my times of frustration, I couldn't understand why God was making me wait whilst others seemed to be leaving me behind. People would pat me on the back and reassure me that, 'my time would come'. I wanted to harm them sometimes (Lord, forgive me) – I didn't want their pity, I wanted my life partner.

In the earlier stages of marriage, there were times that I longed to have my singleness again, and yet I had prayed (and fasted) for years to be married. Does green grass come to mind?

However, I have to hold my hands up and say, if

God had allowed me to get married when I *thought* I was ready.... I probably wouldn't be married now! My marriage would have ended a long, long, time ago. You see, whether you feel you know yourself or not, what you certainly do not know is the person you will be when you are married. I had no idea. I certainly couldn't be the same person I was in my singleness. Everything that you do and say in your marriage affects everyone else in your family. Including your extended family and the family you have just married into. Throw some kids into the mix and you now have a massive melting pot of emotions, needs, desires, dislikes, demands, requests and expectations to contend with. And sometimes, in fact, quite often, you are the focal point, trying to hold it all together. Your needs can often come last after everything else is taken care of, and once everything is taken care of, all you are good for is bed. You land in bed, exhausted and, oh look, there's another demand to be met!

Now, it may sound like I'm painting a picture of doom and gloom – I'm trying to be real with you. I love being married. I also love my own space. I love being a mother. I also love my independence. I have learnt to juggle them all, but I have yet to perfect it all. I probably never will, and I'm okay with that.

My point to you is, know yourself and then get ready to change. If you see the word change as negative, you may struggle in the early stages of relationships and marriage. If you see change as positive, you may thrive as the changes happen. Most of us are somewhere in the middle.

Remain prayerful at all times, giving God the praise and the pain that can come with relationships and marriage.

Set your mind to what is above.

I often asked myself, when I was single, 'What is the difference between Christian marriages and non-Christian marriages? I mean, apart from attending church on Sundays! I was taught, and have found to be true, that my marriage exists to glorify God and His kingdom. That was the realization that stopped Rob and I in our tracks when we were constantly bickering and arguing about nonsense. We realized that we were wasting time and effort that could be used for the body of Christ. Before we were married, we both spent a lot of time serving in our local church in various ministries. Then we got married and seemed to be giving all our time and effort to the ministry of madness!

When a marriage is good and Godly, the offshoots of that marriage will be far reaching. Take a look at those that will be positively affected by a good marriage:

- Each other – Your peace and joy will be displayed for all to see
- Children – They need positive role models to guide and assist them when it's their turn to choose their own spouses
- Your parents – They can be at peace knowing you are in good hands
- Siblings – Have an example to follow in their own relationships
- Neighbours – Have role models to follow, occasional cakes and meals to appreciate and no shouting next door!
- Teachers – Your children's teachers will have pleasant parents to deal with

- Work colleagues – Are inspired when you speak positively about your spouse
- Friends – Are encouraged that there are good marriages out there and will desire the same for themselves
- Strangers – Even if they don't always get the opportunity, will comment on the fact that, 'You are such a lovely couple!'

You carry that responsibility, so you might as well do it well and enjoy it!

Now devote your heart and soul to seeking the Lord your God. Begin to build the sanctuary of the Lord God, so that you may bring the ark of the covenant of the Lord and the sacred articles belonging to God into the temple that will be built for the Name of the Lord.

1 Chronicles 22:19 (NIV)

God instructed me, when I was single, to 'Be a wife before you are a wife!' I had absolutely no idea what He meant at the time, but now I do. Prepare for the gift which is to come before it arrives so that you may be more ready than you think you are now.

Speaking of gifts – do you realize that you are someone's gift? Someone is going to receive *you* one day, and they will be so delighted.

The thing is, when you receive a gift (assuming it is wrapped) you have no idea what is inside, yet you are happy to receive it, right? Generally, it is presented beautifully because somebody has taken the time to wrap it with carefully chosen gift wrap or an appropriate gift box or bag. Inside, there may be layers of tissue paper protecting the gift. Most will carefully open the gift removing each layer slowly and with expectation and anticipation until the gift is revealed.

You do understand though, that a gift is not to be opened until the allocated time, i.e. your birthday, Christmas etc. – so there may be a period of waiting involved once you receive the gift. This, of course, will build the anticipation further, but that is not a bad thing, right?

Well, there are those that just cannot wait and will open the gift before the allocated time. These people may find that they are regretful or disappointed when the allocated time arrives as they already know what is in their gift, because they have opened it. Their celebration doesn't feel the same as the others around them who are busy celebrating with their anticipated gift.

There are also those that will open the gift early and then discard it. They may not like the gift but because it has been opened they can no longer return or exchange it and now they are stuck with it. These gifts tend to get left on the shelf or in a dark cupboard never to be looked at again.

But, those that wait with excitement, but exercise patience and self-control, will open their gift at the allotted time and appreciate not just the gift but also the giver of the gift. Some even keep the wrapping as it reminds them of the beauty with which the gift was given.

You are a priceless, irreplaceable, unique gift and you will be *given* at the right time. Allow God, our creator, to be the *'giver'*.

GOD, *investigate my life;*
get all the facts first-hand.
I'm an open book to you;
even from a distance, you know what I'm thinking.
You know when I leave and when I get back;
I'm never out of your sight.
You know everything I'm going to say
before I start the first sentence.
I look behind me and you're there,
then up ahead and you're there, too—
your reassuring presence, coming and going.
This is too much, too wonderful—
I can't take it all in!

Is there any place I can go to avoid your Spirit?
to be out of your sight?
If I climb to the sky, you're there!
If I go underground, you're there!
If I flew on morning's wings
to the far western horizon,
You'd find me in a minute—
you're already there waiting!
Then I said to myself, "Oh, he even sees me in the
dark!
At night I'm immersed in the light!"
It's a fact: darkness isn't dark to you;
night and day, darkness and light, they're all the
same to you.

Oh yes, you shaped me first inside, then out;
you formed me in my mother's womb.
I thank you, High God—you're breathtaking!
Body and soul, I am marvelously made!
I worship in adoration—what a creation!

You know me inside and out,
you know every bone in my body;
You know exactly how I was made, bit by bit,
how I was sculpted from nothing into something.
Like an open book, you watched me grow from
conception to birth;
all the stages of my life were spread out before you,
The days of my life all prepared
before I'd even lived one day.

Psalm 139: 1-16 (MSG)

For your Maker is your husband—
the LORD Almighty is his name—

Isaiah 54:5 (NIV)

ABOUT THE AUTHOR

Sonia and Rob reside in Essex with their three sons.

Sonia enjoys reading, period dramas, shopping, driving, walking, talking and gourmet jelly beans!

Rob enjoys people, cooking, eating, the gym, football, spas and sleeping.

Together they enjoy their sons, watching movies, five-star hotels and show homes!

CONTACT THE AUTHOR

If you would like to contact the author or you would like the *Rooted for Relationships* course to be held at your establishment, please email:

rootedforrelationships@gmail.com

Printed in Poland
by Amazon Fulfillment
Poland Sp. z o.o., Wrocław

50425214R00145